# Why Men Cheat

## Hidden Reasons Every Wife Should Know

John B. Amayo

# Preface

Welcome to "Why Men Cheat." This book delves into one of the most sensitive and challenging aspects of human relationships: infidelity. Whether you are reading this as someone who has experienced infidelity, as a concerned partner looking to prevent it, or simply as a curious seeker of knowledge, I extend my warmest welcome.

Infidelity is a complex and emotionally charged topic that has the power to profoundly impact individuals, couples, and families. It is a subject often shrouded in secrecy and shame, but it is also a reality that many relationships face. This book aims to shed light on the multifaceted aspects of infidelity, from its causes and consequences to its prevention and healing.

As you journey through these pages, you will find a wealth of insights, guidance, and practical advice. We will explore the different forms of infidelity, the emotional and psychological consequences it brings, and its ripple effect on children and families. You will gain an understanding of why men cheat, touching upon emotional disconnection, sexual dissatisfaction, personal insecurities, and the lure of opportunity.

But this book is not solely about understanding the problem; it is also about finding solutions. You will discover strategies for preventing infidelity, rebuilding trust, and creating a faithful future. We will explore the importance of self-awareness, effective communication, and fostering emotional intimacy in your relationship.

Throughout your journey, keep in mind that every relationship is unique. While this book provides valuable insights and a roadmap for navigating the challenges of infidelity, it is not a one-size-fits-all solution. Your path to healing and strengthening your relationship may require individualized approaches, professional guidance, and patience.

I encourage you to approach this book with an open heart and a willingness to explore the depths of your emotions, desires, and vulnerabilities. Remember that you are not alone in your quest for healthier, happier, and more faithful partnerships. Countless individuals and couples have faced similar challenges and emerged stronger and more resilient.

Ultimately, the aim of this book is to empower you with knowledge, inspire self-reflection, and provide you with the tools to build a love that endures. Whether you are seeking to prevent infidelity, heal from its wounds, or simply understand the complexities of human relationships, may this book be a source of insight, guidance, and hope on your journey.

With warm regards,

John B. Amayo

# Copyright©

# Table of Contents

# PART I: UNDERSTANDING INFIDELITY

# Chapter 1: Introduction

**Introduction:**

**The Hidden Reality of Infidelity**

In the realm of human relationships, few topics evoke as much fear, pain, and uncertainty as infidelity. It is a word that can shatter the very foundation of trust upon which love and partnerships are built. When we hear the word "cheating," a myriad of emotions surge within us – anger, sadness, betrayal, and often, confusion. Why do people cheat? Why, despite the promises and commitments made, do some individuals find themselves drawn to infidelity?

**A Sobering Prevalence**

Infidelity is a pervasive issue that transcends boundaries of age, culture, and social class. It affects not only those directly involved but also ripples through families and communities, leaving a trail of emotional wreckage in its wake. Statistics tell us that a significant percentage of individuals have experienced infidelity in their relationships, either as the one who strayed or as the one who was betrayed. While the numbers alone are alarming, it is the stories behind these statistics that truly highlight the gravity of the issue.

**The Painful Impact**

The consequences of infidelity are far-reaching. Emotional devastation, broken trust, and fractured relationships are just the beginning. Children caught in the crossfire often bear scars that persist into adulthood. Financial and legal complications can further complicate an already distressing situation. Lives are upended, and healing can seem like an insurmountable challenge.

**Empowering Knowledge**

The purpose of this book is to delve into the intricate web of infidelity and shed light on one specific facet: why men cheat. We aim to provide a comprehensive understanding of the hidden reasons behind this behavior. By uncovering the motivations, emotions, and circumstances that lead men to cheat, we empower women with knowledge to protect their relationships.

**A Path to Prevention**

This book is not designed to be a condemnation of men or a justification of infidelity. Instead, it is a journey into the complexities of human relationships. By understanding the root causes and triggers of cheating, we can take proactive steps to safeguard our partnerships. Through open communication, emotional connection, and building trust, we can create relationships that are resilient to the allure of infidelity.

**Your Journey Begins Here**

As you embark on this exploration, keep an open heart and a curious mind. The insights you gain will not only help you understand the motivations behind infidelity but also equip you with tools to strengthen your relationship and prevent cheating from entering your life.

Let us journey together through the pages of "Why Men Cheat: Unveiling the Hidden Reasons and Protecting Your Relationship." Our mission is to empower you with knowledge, guide you through the complexities of infidelity, and ultimately help you build healthier, happier, and more faithful partnerships.

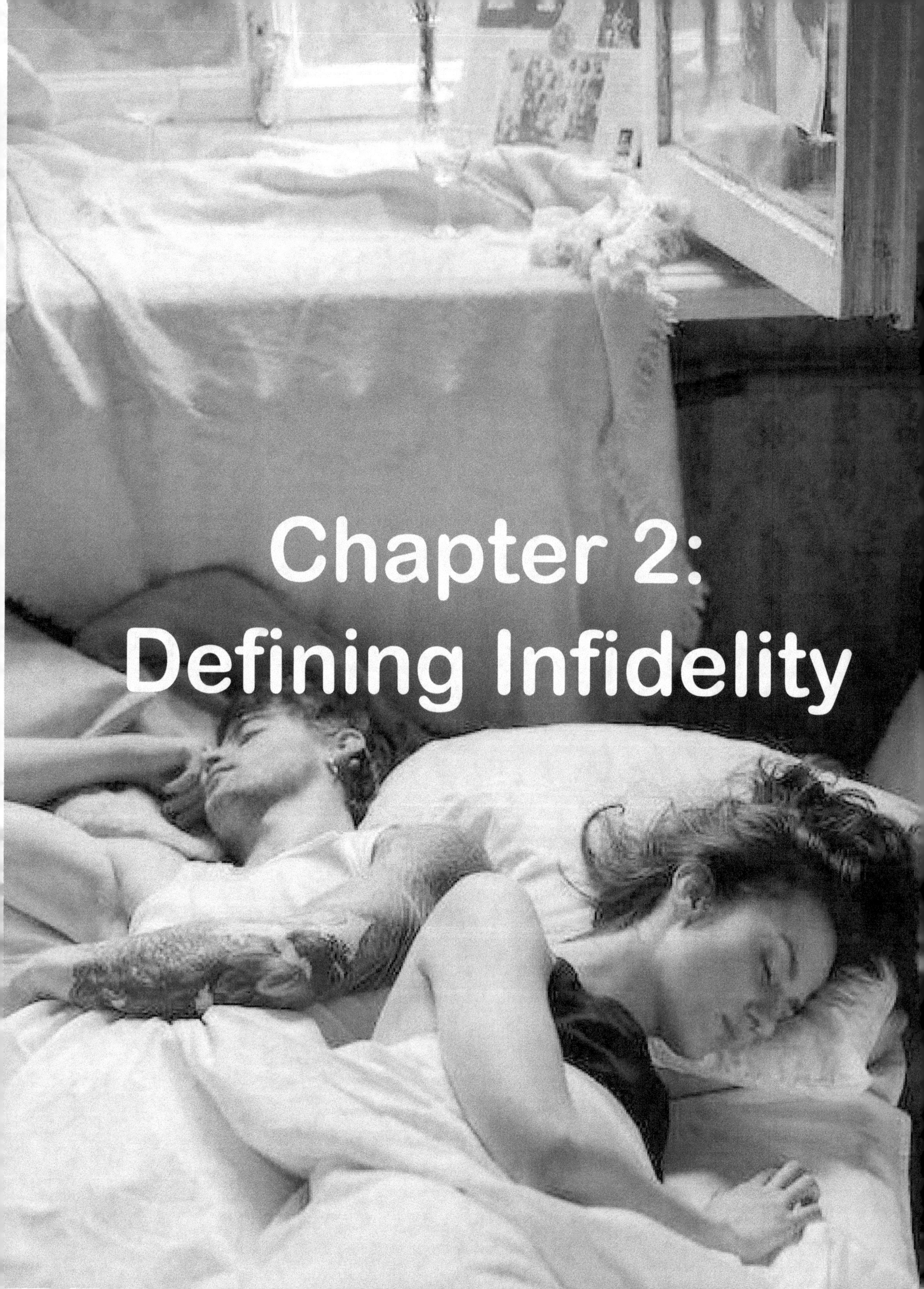

Chapter 2:
Defining Infidelity

# a) Different Forms of Infidelity

Infidelity is a multifaceted concept that extends beyond the confines of a single definition. It encompasses a wide range of behaviors and emotions that can erode the trust and commitment within a romantic relationship. To navigate the intricate landscape of infidelity, it is crucial to first understand the various forms it can take. In this chapter, we will explore the different dimensions of infidelity, shedding light on the complexities that often elude a simplistic definition.

1. **Emotional Infidelity: Beyond the Physical** Infidelity is not limited to physical encounters. Emotional infidelity, often regarded as the precursor to physical cheating, involves forming deep emotional connections with someone outside of the committed relationship. These connections can manifest as intense friendships, secret confidences, or romantic feelings that are not disclosed to the partner.

2. **Physical Infidelity: Crossing the Line** The most commonly recognized form of infidelity, physical cheating, involves engaging in sexual or intimate acts with someone other than one's committed partner. It is the breach of trust that occurs when the boundaries of exclusivity are crossed, leaving emotional scars that can be challenging to heal.

3. **Micro-Cheating: A Gray Area** In the digital age, micro-cheating has emerged as a nuanced form of infidelity. It involves subtle behaviors such as excessive flirting, secretive texting, or maintaining online relationships that, while not overtly sexual, can still undermine trust and emotional fidelity.

4. **Virtual Infidelity: The Online Temptation** The internet has opened up new avenues for infidelity to flourish. Virtual infidelity occurs when individuals engage in romantic or sexual interactions exclusively online, often with people they have never met in person. It blurs the lines between physical and emotional infidelity, posing unique challenges to committed relationships.

5. **Financial Infidelity: Secrets in the Bank** Money matters can also be a breeding ground for infidelity. Financial infidelity occurs when one partner hides financial transactions, assets, or debts from the other. This breach of trust can have far-reaching consequences, both financial and emotional.

**Recognizing the Signs**

Understanding the different forms of infidelity is the first step in recognizing its presence in your relationship. In the subsequent chapters, we will explore the signs and red flags associated with each form, helping you become more attuned to potential infidelity in your partnership.

As we embark on this journey of understanding infidelity, remember that it is a complex and deeply emotional issue. By unraveling its dimensions, we equip ourselves with the knowledge needed to navigate the challenges it presents and, ultimately, to protect and strengthen our relationships.

# b) Emotional vs. Physical Infidelity

In the intricate landscape of infidelity, two primary categories often stand out: emotional infidelity and physical infidelity. Each of these forms of infidelity carries its own unique set of dynamics, consequences, and challenges. Let us delve deeper into these two categories and understand their distinctions through real-life examples.

**(i) Emotional Infidelity: The Heart's Betrayal**

Emotional infidelity involves forming deep emotional connections with someone outside of the committed relationship. While there may not be physical intimacy, the emotional intensity can rival or even surpass that of the primary partnership. Here are some examples:

1. **Intimate Confidant:** Mark, a married man, regularly confides in his female coworker, Lisa, about his deepest fears and aspirations. They share secrets, offer emotional support, and turn to each other when facing life's challenges. While they haven't engaged in physical intimacy, the emotional bond they share crosses boundaries.

2. **Long-Distance Emotional Affair:** Sarah, in a long-distance relationship with her partner, finds solace in an online friend she's never met in person. They exchange heartfelt messages, share dreams, and provide each other with the emotional connection missing from her relationship.

3. **Rekindled Romance:** After reconnecting with an old flame on social media, Maria starts communicating with him secretly. They reminisce about their past and share romantic fantasies. Although they haven't met in person, the emotional affair threatens her commitment to her current partner.

**(ii) Physical Infidelity: Crossing Boundaries**

Physical infidelity is perhaps the most commonly recognized form of cheating. It involves engaging in sexual or intimate acts with someone other than one's committed partner. Here are some examples:

1. **One-Night Stand:** John, who is married, goes on a business trip and succumbs to temptation, having a one-night stand with a colleague while away from his spouse.

2. **Secret Affair:** Laura embarks on a passionate, ongoing affair with her neighbor, Tom, unbeknownst to her partner. They meet in secret and engage in sexual activities, which she hides from her committed relationship.

3. **Extramarital Relationship:** Mike becomes involved in a full-fledged romantic and sexual relationship with a woman he met through a mutual hobby group. He maintains this relationship alongside his marriage, juggling two commitments simultaneously.

**The Blurred Lines and Overlaps**

It is essential to recognize that the lines between emotional and physical infidelity can sometimes blur. Emotional infidelity, if left unchecked, can lead to physical infidelity, as emotional bonds often create a pathway to physical intimacy. Likewise, physical infidelity can generate intense emotional turmoil for all parties involved. These two forms of infidelity are interconnected and often reinforce each other, making it crucial to address both aspects when dealing with relationship challenges.

As we move forward in our exploration of infidelity, remember that both emotional and physical infidelity can inflict significant harm on a relationship. Recognizing the signs and understanding the nuances of each form are essential steps toward preserving the trust and intimacy within your partnership.

## c) Recognizing the Signs of Cheating

Infidelity, whether emotional or physical, often leaves behind a trail of telltale signs. While these signs are not foolproof evidence of cheating, they can serve as red flags that warrant further exploration and communication within the relationship. It is essential to approach these signs with sensitivity and open dialogue. Here is a list of specific signs of cheating to be aware of:

1. **Emotional Distance:** A sudden and unexplained emotional distance between you and your partner can be a sign of emotional infidelity. If they become more secretive about their thoughts and feelings, it may indicate that they are sharing them with someone else.

2. **Increased Secrecy:** If your partner starts hiding their phone, sets a password, or becomes defensive about their privacy, it could be a sign of either emotional or physical infidelity.

3. **Change in Communication Patterns:** Noticeable changes in communication, such as fewer phone calls, fewer messages, or reluctance to discuss their day, might indicate that your partner is investing their emotional energy elsewhere.

4. **Defensiveness:** A defensive reaction when questioned about their activities, friends, or whereabouts can be a sign that your partner is hiding something.

5. **Excessive Time Away:** Frequent and unexplained absences or spending more time away from home, especially if they claim work-related reasons, could raise suspicion.

6. **Loss of Interest in Intimacy:** A sudden decline in interest in physical intimacy or a noticeable change in your sexual relationship may signal emotional or physical infidelity.

7. **New or Secretive Friendships:** If your partner develops close friendships with someone you have never met or heard of and is secretive about their interactions, it is a potential red flag.

8. **Change in Appearance or Grooming:** A sudden desire to improve physical appearance, dressing differently, or grooming excessively may indicate an attempt to impress or attract someone new.

9. **Unexplained Expenses:** Large, unexplained expenditures, hidden credit card bills, or financial secrecy can be indicative of financial infidelity, which often goes hand-in-hand with emotional or physical infidelity.

10. **Change in Routine:** If your partner starts altering their daily routine without a reasonable explanation, it may be a sign that they are making time for someone else.

11. **Gut Feeling:** Trust your instincts. If something does not feel right in your relationship, and you sense that your partner may be cheating, it is crucial to address your concerns in a healthy and constructive manner.

12. **Unexplained Absences During Important Events:** Missing important family gatherings, holidays, or anniversaries without a reasonable excuse can be a clear sign of a partner's emotional or physical detachment.

13. **Excessive Defensive Statements:** When your partner excessively defends the idea of privacy, insisting on the importance of individual space in the relationship, it may indicate they are guarding secrets.

14. **Changes in Social Media Behavior:** A sudden increase in social media activity, especially private messaging with someone unfamiliar to you, can be a sign of emotional infidelity.

15. **Inconsistent Stories:** If your partner provides inconsistent or conflicting explanations for their actions or whereabouts, it is a potential indicator of deceit.

Remember that these signs should not be used to jump to conclusions or accuse your partner without evidence. Open and honest communication is the most effective way to address concerns about infidelity in your relationship. If you notice several of these signs and have reason to suspect cheating, consider discussing your concerns with your partner in a non-confrontational manner to gain clarity and work toward resolution.

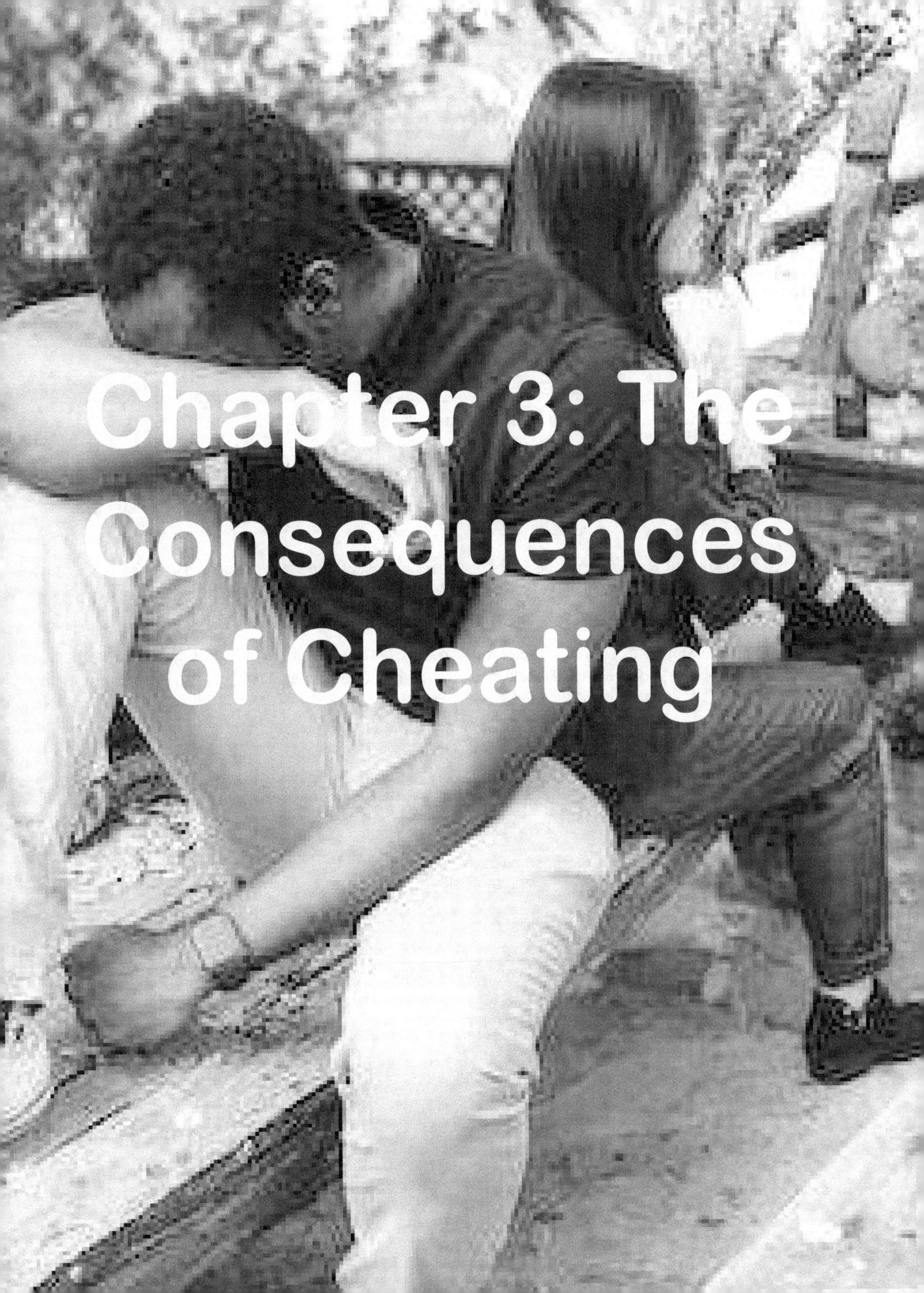
Chapter 3: The Consequences of Cheating

# a) Emotional, Psychological, and Relational Consequences

The act of cheating in a romantic relationship is not without profound consequences. It leaves an indelible mark on the individuals involved and can have far-reaching effects on their emotional well-being, psychological state, and the dynamics of the relationship itself. In this chapter, we will explore the multifaceted consequences of cheating, including the emotional turmoil, psychological distress, and relational fallout that often follow.

**Emotional Consequences:**

1. **Betrayal and Hurt:** For the person who has been cheated on, the overwhelming feeling is one of betrayal and deep emotional pain. The sense of trust, which forms the foundation of any healthy relationship, is shattered.

2. **Low Self-Esteem:** Cheating can lead to a sharp decline in self-esteem, causing the betrayed individual to question their worth and desirability. They may wonder what they lacked that led their partner to cheat.

3. **Anger and Resentment:** Feelings of anger and resentment are common reactions to infidelity. The person who was cheated on often struggles to cope with the injustice of their partner's actions.

4. **Depression and Anxiety:** The emotional toll of infidelity can manifest as symptoms of depression and anxiety. The betrayed individual may experience sleep disturbances, loss of appetite, and persistent worry.

**Psychological Consequences:**

1. **Trust Issues:** After experiencing infidelity, individuals often develop deep-seated trust issues. This can extend beyond their current relationship and affect their ability to trust others in the future.

2. **Post-Traumatic Stress:** In some cases, infidelity can lead to symptoms akin to post-traumatic stress disorder (PTSD), including flashbacks, hypervigilance, and emotional numbness.

3. **Obsessive Thoughts:** The discovery of cheating can lead to obsessive thoughts about the betrayal. Intrusive images and constant rumination about the infidelity are not uncommon.

4. **Loss of Identity:** Some individuals tie their identity closely to their relationships. Infidelity can lead to a loss of identity, as they grapple with the profound changes in their self-concept.

**Relational Consequences:**

1. **Breakdown of Trust:** Trust, once broken, is challenging to rebuild. The trust between partners is often fractured, leading to a sense of insecurity and instability in the relationship.

2. **Communication Breakdown:** Infidelity can create a significant breakdown in communication between partners. Honest and open dialogue becomes more difficult, as both parties may fear confrontation or further emotional pain.

3. **Potential End of the Relationship:** In many cases, infidelity serves as the catalyst for the dissolution of the relationship. The betrayed partner may choose to end the relationship due to an inability to forgive or rebuild trust.

4. **Impact on Children:** If children are involved, infidelity can have a lasting impact on their emotional well-being. Witnessing the discord and potential separation of their parents can be deeply traumatic.

5. **Rebuilding or Transformation:** In some instances, couples choose to work through the aftermath of infidelity, embarking on a difficult journey of rebuilding trust and healing their relationship. This process can lead to profound transformation if both partners are committed to growth and change.

Understanding the emotional, psychological, and relational consequences of cheating is crucial for individuals who have experienced it and for those who seek to prevent it in their relationships. The aftermath of infidelity is not to be underestimated, and addressing these consequences requires empathy, communication, and often professional support to facilitate healing and growth.

# b) The Ripple Effect on Children and Families

Infidelity is not a private matter confined to the individuals directly involved; it has a profound ripple effect that extends to the wider family, including children. In this section, we will explore how cheating can impact children and families, shedding light on the emotional and psychological challenges that arise in these complex situations.

**1. Emotional Turmoil for Children:**

- **Confusion and Betrayal:** Children often feel confused and betrayed when they discover that one of their parents has cheated. They may question their understanding of love, commitment, and trust.

- **Anger and Resentment:** Older children, in particular, may experience anger and resentment toward the parent who cheated, blaming them for the pain and disruption caused to the family.

- **Emotional Distress:** The turmoil in the family can lead to emotional distress in children, including symptoms of anxiety, depression, and difficulty in concentrating at school.

**2. Altered Family Dynamics:**

- **Parental Conflict:** The discovery of infidelity can lead to heightened conflict between the parents. Frequent arguments and tension can create a hostile living environment for everyone in the family.

- **Change in Caregiving Roles:** Infidelity can lead to changes in caregiving roles, with one parent potentially moving out or emotional distance between the parents affecting their ability to co-parent effectively.

- **Loss of Stability:** The sense of stability and security that children rely on can be disrupted when infidelity leads to parental separation or divorce.

**3. Impact on Future Relationships:**

- **Modeling Unhealthy Behavior:** Children may unwittingly model unhealthy relationship behavior they observe in their parents, including a skewed understanding of trust and commitment.

- **Difficulty in Trusting:** Children who witness infidelity may have difficulty trusting others in their future relationships. They may carry the fear of betrayal into their own romantic endeavors.

**4. Coping Mechanisms:**

- **Withdrawal:** Some children may withdraw emotionally or physically from the family, attempting to distance themselves from the turmoil.

- **Seeking Support:** Others may seek support outside the family, turning to friends, teachers, or counselors to help them navigate their feelings.

**5. Long-term Effects:**

- **Potential for Resilience:** While infidelity can have immediate and long-lasting consequences, it is important to note that some children and families exhibit remarkable resilience and can eventually find healing and growth through therapy and support.

- **Extended Family Impact:** Infidelity can also impact the extended family, as grandparents, aunts, uncles, and cousins may become involved or affected by the fallout.

Recognizing the ripple effect of infidelity on children and families underscores the importance of addressing the issue promptly and responsibly. Open communication, seeking professional help, and prioritizing the emotional well-being of children are crucial steps in mitigating the impact of cheating on the family unit. In cases where reconciliation is not possible, fostering a healthy co-parenting relationship can provide stability and support to children during challenging times.

# c) The High Cost of Infidelity

Infidelity exacts a significant toll, not just emotionally and psychologically but also in practical and tangible ways. The financial, legal, and societal costs associated with cheating can be substantial. In this section, we will explore the high cost of infidelity from multiple angles, emphasizing the real-world impact it can have on individuals and couples.

**1. Financial Consequences:**

- **Divorce and Alimony:** Infidelity is often cited as a leading cause of divorce. In many divorce cases, infidelity can influence the division of assets and the determination of alimony payments. Legal fees associated with divorce can also be substantial.

- **Child Support:** When children are involved, child support payments may be mandated by the court. These financial obligations can place a strain on the income and financial stability of the parent responsible for making payments.

- **Marital Assets:** The process of dividing marital assets, including property, investments, and savings, can become complicated and contentious when infidelity is a factor.

**2. Legal Consequences:**

- **Adultery Laws:** In some jurisdictions, adultery is still considered a criminal offense, although prosecutions are rare. However, it can be used as evidence in divorce proceedings and custody battles.

- **Child Custody:** Infidelity can impact child custody arrangements, with the court considering factors such as the impact of the affair on the children and the moral fitness of the parents.

- **Prenuptial Agreements:** Prenuptial agreements often contain clauses related to infidelity, specifying the financial consequences if one spouse cheats.

**3. Emotional and Psychological Costs:**

- **Therapy and Counseling:** Many couples seek therapy or counseling to address the emotional fallout of infidelity. These sessions can be costly, both in terms of time and money.

- **Individual Therapy:** Both the person who cheated and the one who was betrayed may require individual therapy to cope with the emotional trauma and navigate the healing process.

**4. Impact on Reputation:**

- **Social Stigma:** Infidelity can carry a social stigma that can affect a person's reputation within their community or social circles.

- **Professional Consequences:** In certain professions, an individual's moral character may be closely scrutinized. Infidelity can lead to professional consequences, including damage to one's career or reputation.

## 5. Health-Related Costs:

- **Sexually Transmitted Infections (STIs):** Engaging in unprotected sexual activity outside the committed relationship can lead to the transmission of STIs, necessitating medical treatment and ongoing healthcare costs.

## 6. Impact on Future Relationships:

- **Trust Issues:** Individuals who have experienced infidelity in previous relationships may carry trust issues into future relationships, potentially impacting their ability to form healthy, trusting partnerships.

It is important to note that the high cost of infidelity is not limited to monetary expenses or legal consequences. The emotional and psychological toll on all parties involved can be immeasurable. While some couples can work through the challenges and rebuild their relationships, others may ultimately decide that the cost of staying together outweighs the benefits.

Understanding the multifaceted costs of infidelity underscores the importance of maintaining open communication, seeking professional help when needed, and taking proactive steps to nurture healthy, faithful, and fulfilling relationships. Prevention is often far less costly, both emotionally and financially, than dealing with the aftermath of infidelity.

PART II:
EXPLORING THE
ROOT CAUSES

# Chapter 4: Lack of Emotional Connection

# a) The Importance of Emotional Intimacy

Emotional intimacy lies at the heart of any healthy, fulfilling, and enduring romantic relationship. It is the foundation upon which trust, vulnerability, and genuine connection are built. In this chapter, we will delve into the profound significance of emotional intimacy and why it plays a pivotal role in preventing infidelity.

**1. Building Trust:**

- **Trust is the Cornerstone:** Trust is the bedrock of a strong relationship. Emotional intimacy fosters trust as partners share their innermost thoughts, feelings, and vulnerabilities with each other.

- **Predictability and Reliability:** Emotional intimacy allows partners to predict each other's responses and rely on each other for emotional support, creating a sense of safety and security within the relationship.

**2. Fostering Open Communication:**

- **A Safe Space to Express:** Emotional intimacy creates a safe space where partners can express their thoughts, concerns, and desires without fear of judgment or rejection.

- **Conflict Resolution:** In emotionally intimate relationships, conflicts are less likely to escalate because partners feel comfortable discussing their issues openly and working together to find solutions.

**3. Strengthening Connection:**

- **Deep Connection:** Emotional intimacy enables partners to connect on a deeper level. It is this emotional closeness that differentiates a romantic partnership from other relationships.

- **Emotional Bonds:** Sharing vulnerabilities and emotions creates strong emotional bonds that enhance the sense of togetherness and commitment.

**4. Fulfilling Emotional Needs:**

- **Emotional Fulfillment:** Emotional intimacy ensures that partners meet each other's emotional needs. Feeling heard, understood, and supported by one's partner is essential for emotional well-being.

- **Preventing Emotional Neglect:** In the absence of emotional intimacy, one or both partners may seek emotional fulfillment outside the relationship, inadvertently opening the door to infidelity.

**5. Safeguarding Against Infidelity:**

- **A Deterrent to Cheating:** Emotional intimacy acts as a deterrent to cheating. When partners feel emotionally connected and fulfilled within their relationship, they are less likely to seek emotional connection elsewhere.

- **Creating Resilience:** A relationship rich in emotional intimacy is more resilient to the challenges that life throws its way. Couples who share a strong emotional bond are better equipped to weather storms together.

**6. Nurturing and Maintaining Emotional Intimacy:**

- **Quality Time:** Spending quality time together is essential for maintaining emotional intimacy. Engage in activities you both enjoy and create opportunities for meaningful conversations.

- **Active Listening:** Practice active listening by giving your partner your full attention and validating their feelings and experiences.

- **Expressing Love and Appreciation:** Regularly express your love, gratitude, and appreciation for your partner. Small gestures of affection can go a long way in nurturing emotional intimacy.

- **Seeking Professional Help:** If emotional intimacy has waned in your relationship, consider seeking the guidance of a relationship therapist or counselor to help you rebuild it.

In summary, emotional intimacy is not merely a desirable aspect of a relationship; it is a fundamental necessity for preventing infidelity and creating a strong, enduring partnership. By prioritizing emotional connection, couples can fortify their relationship against the allure of emotional or physical infidelity and enjoy a deeper, more fulfilling bond.

# b) How Emotional Neglect Can Lead to Infidelity

Emotional neglect within a relationship can create a fertile breeding ground for infidelity. When one or both partners feel emotionally unfulfilled or ignored, they may seek solace, validation, and connection elsewhere. In this section, we'll explore how emotional neglect can lead to infidelity and the underlying mechanisms behind this phenomenon.

**1. Seeking Emotional Fulfillment:**

- **Unmet Needs:** When a partner's emotional needs are consistently unmet or ignored within the relationship, they may look for emotional fulfillment elsewhere. This can be through friendships, online relationships, or extramarital affairs.

- **Feeling Undervalued:** Emotional neglect can make individuals feel undervalued, unimportant, or invisible within their own relationship. Seeking validation from someone else can provide a sense of worth.

**2. Vulnerability to Temptation:**

- **Validation and Attention:** External sources of validation and attention can be enticing. When someone offers the emotional connection that is lacking within the relationship, it can be difficult to resist.

- **Escapism:** Emotional neglect can create feelings of isolation and frustration. Infidelity may be seen as a form of escape from the emotional void at home.

## 3. Emotional Affairs:

- **Emotional Infidelity:** Emotional affairs involve forming deep emotional connections with someone other than one's committed partner. These connections may start innocently but can quickly escalate into romantic or sexual infidelity.

- **Bonding Over Shared Neglect:** Partners engaging in emotional affairs often bond over shared feelings of emotional neglect within their respective relationships. This shared experience can intensify their connection.

## 4. Coping Mechanism:

- **Emotional Coping:** For some individuals, infidelity becomes a way to cope with the emotional pain and emptiness they experience in their primary relationship. The excitement and attention of a new relationship can serve as a distraction.

- **Temporary Relief:** The emotional connection experienced outside the relationship may provide temporary relief from the feelings of loneliness and dissatisfaction within the primary partnership.

## 5. Lack of Communication:

- **Silent Suffering:** In emotionally neglectful relationships, partners may avoid addressing the issue due to fear of conflict or further emotional distance. This silence can perpetuate the cycle of neglect.

- **Failure to Recognize the Impact:** Sometimes, partners may not even realize the extent of emotional neglect or the impact it has on their relationship until it is too late.

## 6. Building Emotional Resilience:

- **Open Communication:** The key to preventing emotional neglect from leading to infidelity is open and honest communication. Partners must be willing to discuss their emotional needs and concerns.

- **Therapy and Counseling:** Seeking professional help through couples therapy or counseling can provide a safe space to address and resolve emotional neglect within the relationship.

- **Quality Time and Connection:** Prioritizing quality time together and actively working to rebuild emotional intimacy can strengthen the bond between partners.

In conclusion, emotional neglect is a potent precursor to infidelity. Recognizing the signs of emotional neglect within a relationship and addressing it proactively is essential to prevent the erosion of emotional intimacy and the potential for infidelity. By prioritizing emotional connection and fulfillment within the relationship, couples can create a strong and resilient partnership that withstands the allure of infidelity.

# c) Building and Maintaining Emotional Connections

Building and maintaining emotional connections in a relationship is vital to prevent emotional neglect and infidelity. Emotional intimacy requires effort and commitment from both partners. Here are some practical examples of how a wife can build and maintain an emotional connection with her husband within the context of their home:

**1. Quality Conversations:**

- **Daily Check-Ins:** Set aside time each day for meaningful conversations. Ask your husband about his day, his thoughts, and how he's feeling. Be an active and empathetic listener.

- **Create Conversation Spaces:** Designate comfortable spaces in your home, like a cozy living room nook or a porch swing, where you can have uninterrupted, heart-to-heart conversations.

**2. Shared Interests:**

- **Shared Hobbies:** Find activities or hobbies that you both enjoy and can do together at home. Whether it is cooking, gardening, painting, or DIY projects, shared interests create opportunities for bonding.

- **Date Nights at Home:** Plan regular date nights at home. Cook a special meal together, set the table with candles, and create a romantic ambiance to nurture your emotional connection.

**3. Affection and Physical Touch:**

- **Physical Affection:** Offer hugs, kisses, and physical touch throughout the day to express love and affection. Physical connection fosters emotional closeness.

- **Bedtime Rituals:** Establish bedtime routines that involve cuddling, talking, or simply holding hands before falling asleep.

**4. Acts of Kindness:**

- **Surprise Gestures:** Surprise your husband with thoughtful gestures, such as leaving love notes around the house, preparing his favorite snacks, or making his morning coffee.

- **Acts of Service:** Show your love by helping with household chores or tasks, relieving some of his stress and allowing more time for emotional connection.

**5. Supportive Environment:**

- **Create a Safe Space:** Ensure that your home is a safe, judgment-free zone where your husband feels comfortable expressing his thoughts, feelings, and vulnerabilities.

- **Conflict Resolution:** Address conflicts and disagreements calmly and constructively, focusing on finding solutions together rather than escalating tensions.

**6. Technology-Free Zones:**

- **Designate Tech-Free Times:** Establish specific times or zones within your home where technology is put aside. This allows for uninterrupted face-to-face interaction.

**7. Nurturing Shared Dreams:**

- **Vision Board:** Create a vision board together that showcases your shared goals, dreams, and aspirations. It is a visual reminder of your emotional connection and the future you are building together.

**8. Gratitude and Appreciation:**

- **Daily Gratitude:** Cultivate a practice of daily gratitude by sharing things you appreciate about each other. This reinforces positive feelings and strengthens the emotional bond.

**9. Personal Space and Independence:**

- **Respect Personal Space:** While emotional connection is essential, respecting each other's need for personal space and independence is equally important. Ensure that both partners have time and space for their individual pursuits and self-reflection.

**10. Seek Professional Guidance:**

- **Therapy or Counseling:** If you find it challenging to build or maintain emotional intimacy, consider seeking the assistance of a relationship therapist or counselor. Professional guidance can help you address underlying issues and develop strategies for emotional connection.

Remember that building and maintaining emotional connections in a relationship is an ongoing process that requires dedication, communication, and mutual effort. By creating a nurturing environment within your home, you can strengthen the emotional bond with your husband and fortify your relationship against the risk of emotional neglect and infidelity.

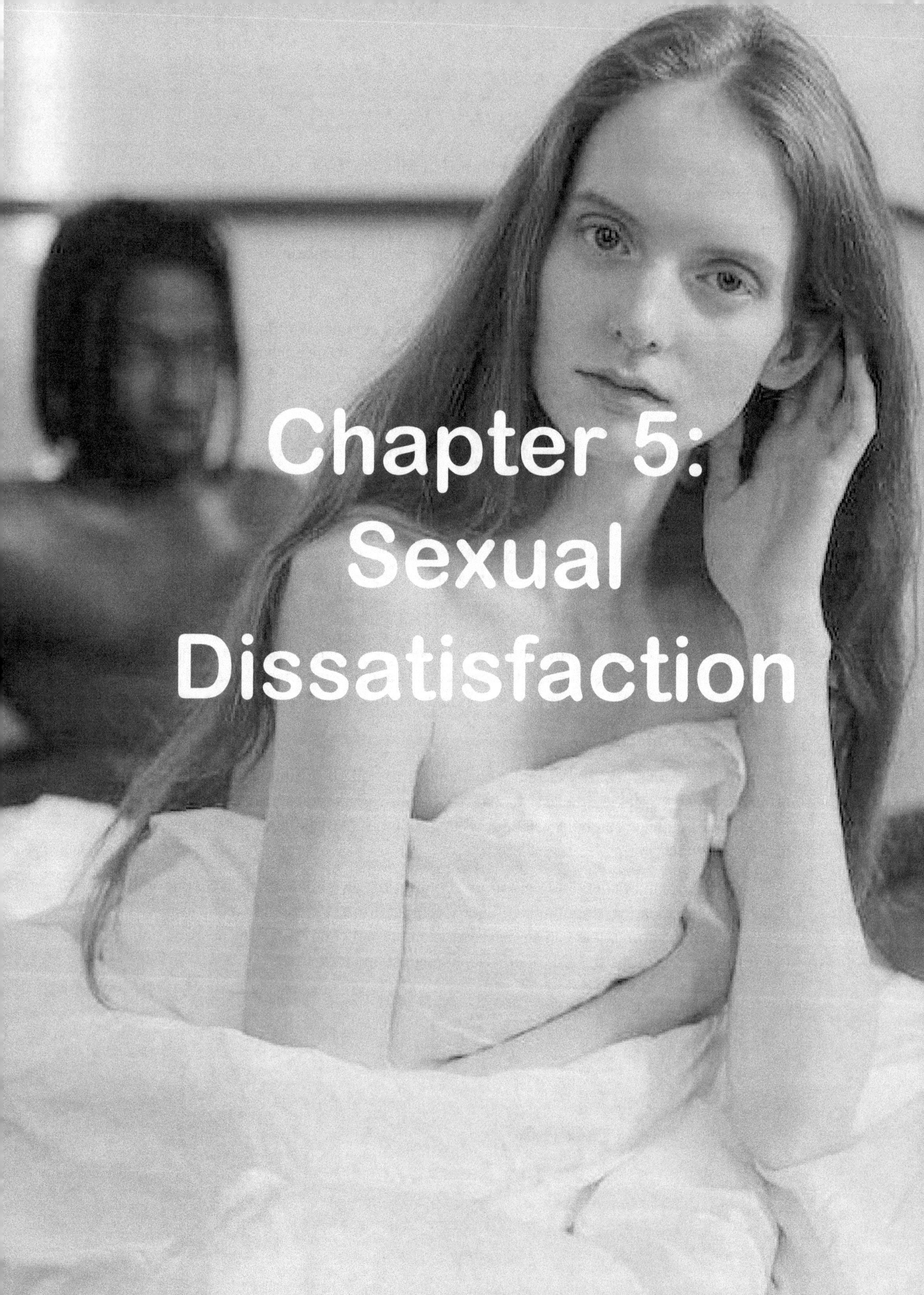

Chapter 5:
Sexual
Dissatisfaction

# a) Meeting Men's Sexual Needs

Understanding men's sexual desires, patterns, and needs requires a nuanced perspective that considers both biological and psychological factors. It is essential to recognize that not all men have the same sexual desires, and individual preferences can vary widely. However, we can explore some general patterns and factors that may contribute to men's sexual desires based on scientific research.

## 1. Biological Factors:

- **Hormonal Influence:** Testosterone, the primary male sex hormone, plays a significant role in men's sexual desire. It is responsible for stimulating sexual thoughts and behaviors. Men generally have higher levels of testosterone than women, which can contribute to their daily sexual desire.

- **Circadian Rhythms:** Research suggests that men often experience peaks in testosterone levels in the morning, leading to a natural inclination for morning erections and heightened sexual desire during this time.

- **Evolutionary Perspective:** From an evolutionary standpoint, men are driven to seek sexual encounters to maximize their reproductive success. This drive may contribute to a frequent desire for sex.

## 2. Psychological and Emotional Factors:

- **Psychological Arousal:** Men's sexual desire is often influenced by psychological factors such as visual stimuli, erotic fantasies, or the anticipation of sexual encounters.

- **Emotional Connection:** Emotional intimacy and connection with a partner can significantly enhance men's sexual desire. Feeling loved, desired, and emotionally connected can be powerful aphrodisiacs.

- **Variety and Novelty:** Some men may have a strong desire for novelty and variety in their sexual experiences. This desire can lead to a preference for frequent sexual activity with a variety of partners or sexual fantasies.

## 3. Relationship Factors:

- **Frequency and Satisfaction:** The frequency of sexual activity can vary among individuals and couples. Men who report a high degree of sexual satisfaction within their relationship may be more motivated to engage in sex frequently.

- **Communication:** Open and honest communication about sexual desires and preferences within a relationship can lead to greater sexual satisfaction and a better understanding of each partner's needs.

## 4. Cultural and Societal Influences:

- **Media and Society:** Cultural and societal norms, as well as media portrayal of sexual relationships, can shape men's perceptions of what is considered "normal" or desirable in terms of sexual frequency.

- **Peer Pressure:** Social circles and peer groups can influence men's sexual desires and behaviors. The desire to conform to perceived norms within one's peer group can affect sexual activity patterns.

It is important to emphasize that not all men need to have sex daily, and there is significant individual variability. Men's sexual desires can change over time due to factors such as age, health, stress, and relationship dynamics. Additionally, men's sexual desires can and should be discussed openly within a relationship to ensure that both partners' needs are met and that there is mutual satisfaction.

Lastly, it is crucial to recognize that sexual desire and satisfaction are not solely determined by biological factors but are shaped by a complex interplay of biology, psychology, emotions, and social influences. Building a fulfilling sexual relationship often requires communication, understanding, and a willingness to adapt to each partner's changing needs and desires.

## b) Situations A Wife May Deny Her Husband Sex

It is important to approach this topic with sensitivity and respect for the complexities of intimate relationships. There can be various reasons why a wife might deny her husband sex, and it is essential to remember that every situation is unique. Here are some specific examples of situations where a wife might deny her husband sex:

1. **Physical or Mental Health Issues:** A wife may be dealing with physical health problems, such as chronic pain, illness, or hormonal imbalances, which can diminish her desire for sex. Mental health issues like depression, anxiety, or past trauma can also affect a person's interest in sexual activity.

2. **Stress and Relationship Problems:** High levels of stress, unresolved conflicts, or communication issues within the marriage can lead to a lack of intimacy. Feelings of anger, resentment, or emotional distance can also impact a couple's sexual relationship.

3. **Fatigue and Lack of Energy:** Exhaustion from work, childcare, or other responsibilities can leave both partners feeling too tired for sex. This can be particularly common in couples with young children.

4. **Medication:** Certain medications can have side effects that reduce libido or sexual desire. If a wife is taking such medications, it can impact her interest in sex.

5. **Mismatched Libidos:** Sometimes, partners in a relationship have differing levels of sexual desire. If a wife has a lower libido than her husband, it can lead to situations where she denies sex more often.

6. **Body Image and Self-Esteem:** Insecurity about one's body or self-esteem issues can affect a person's willingness to engage in sexual activity. This may lead to a wife denying her husband's advances.

7. **Emotional Connection:** A strong emotional connection is often essential for women to feel comfortable and interested in sexual intimacy. If the emotional bond in the relationship is weakened or strained, a wife may deny sex.

8. **Religious or Cultural Beliefs:** Some couples may have religious or cultural beliefs that influence their views on sex. In such cases, a wife might deny sex due to personal convictions or cultural norms.

9. **Previous Negative Sexual Experiences:** Past traumatic or negative sexual experiences can create psychological barriers to intimacy, leading a wife to deny sex.

10. **Infidelity or Betrayal:** Discovering infidelity or feeling betrayed in the relationship can lead to emotional pain and a loss of trust, which can result in a wife denying sex.

It is crucial to approach these situations with empathy and open communication. If a couple is experiencing difficulties in their sexual relationship, seeking professional help from a therapist or counselor who specializes in sexual or relationship issues can be a beneficial step in addressing the underlying causes and finding solutions that work for both partners. Open and honest communication is key to understanding each other's needs and working through any challenges.

## c) How You Can Meet You Husband's Sexual Needs

In nurturing a satisfying sexual relationship with your husband, there are various ways to address his sexual needs and alleviate any feelings of pressure. While it is important to remember that individual preferences can vary greatly, here are some general examples of what wives can do to support their husbands in this regard:

**1. Open Communication:**

- **Encourage Dialogue:** Foster open and honest communication about your sexual desires, boundaries, and fantasies. Create a safe space for both of you to express your needs and preferences without judgment.

- **Active Listening:** Pay close attention to your husband's desires and concerns. Listen actively to understand his perspective and emotions regarding your sexual relationship.

**2. Emotional Connection:**

- **Build Emotional Intimacy:** Strengthen the emotional connection between you and your husband. Make an effort to express love, appreciation, and affection outside of the bedroom.

- **Engage in Quality Time:** Spend quality time together, engage in activities you both enjoy, and create opportunities for bonding and connection.

### 3. Variety and Exploration:

- **Explore Together:** Be open to exploring new experiences, fantasies, and desires with your husband. Experimentation and novelty can add excitement and satisfaction to your sexual relationship.

- **Discuss Fantasies:** Encourage conversations about sexual fantasies and desires. Understanding each other's fantasies and preferences can lead to a more fulfilling sexual connection.

### 4. Reducing Stress and Pressure:

- **Stress Management:** Recognize that stress can have a significant impact on sexual desire. Support your husband in managing stress through relaxation techniques, exercise, or stress-reduction activities.

- **No Pressure Environment:** Create an environment where there is no pressure to perform sexually. Understanding that sexual desire can fluctuate and respecting your husband's boundaries can relieve any feelings of sexual pressure.

### 5. Physical Affection:

- **Physical Connection:** Engage in physical affection outside of sexual encounters. Non-sexual physical touch, such as cuddling, holding hands, and hugging, can nurture intimacy and emotional connection.

- **Initiate Affection:** Take the initiative to show affection and desire for your husband. Express your physical attraction and desire for him in ways that make him feel desired.

### 6. Seek Professional Guidance:

- **Couples Therapy:** If you encounter persistent challenges in meeting each other's sexual needs or if there are unresolved issues, consider seeking the assistance of a qualified couples therapist or sex therapist.

### 7. Respect Boundaries:

- **Establish Boundaries:** Discuss and establish boundaries that are comfortable for both of you. Ensure that you both feel respected and safe within your sexual relationship.

- **Consent:** Always prioritize consent and mutual agreement in sexual activities. Both partners should feel comfortable and enthusiastic about any sexual encounters.

Remember that the key to a satisfying sexual relationship lies in open communication, emotional connection, and mutual respect. Tailoring your approach to your husband's individual preferences and desires will help create a supportive and fulfilling sexual connection that benefits both partners.

# d) The Role of Sexual Compatibility

Sexual compatibility is a crucial factor in a satisfying and fulfilling sexual relationship between partners. It refers to the degree to which two individuals' sexual preferences, desires, and needs align harmoniously. Understanding and fostering sexual compatibility can significantly contribute to preventing sexual dissatisfaction. In this section, we will explore the importance of sexual compatibility and how it influences a couple's sexual satisfaction.

**1. Shared Sexual Preferences:**

- **Compatibility in Desires:** Sexual compatibility involves sharing similar sexual desires and preferences. Partners who have compatible desires are more likely to experience mutual satisfaction and fulfillment.

- **Alignment in Frequency:** Having a similar level of sexual desire and frequency of sexual activity is vital. Mismatches in this area can lead to dissatisfaction and frustration.

**2. Open Communication:**

- **Discussing Desires:** Couples with sexual compatibility are typically more comfortable discussing their sexual desires openly and honestly. This communication allows them to understand each other's needs and boundaries.

- **Resolving Differences:** Even in sexually compatible relationships, differences may arise. Effective communication and problem-solving skills enable partners to address and resolve these differences constructively.

**3. Emotional Connection:**

- **Emotional Intimacy:** Emotional connection plays a crucial role in sexual compatibility. Partners who feel emotionally close are often more sexually satisfied because they can trust and be vulnerable with each other.

- **Enhanced Sensuality:** Emotional intimacy enhances the sensuality of the sexual experience, leading to greater overall satisfaction.

**4. Variety and Exploration:**

- **Willingness to Explore:** Sexually compatible partners are often more willing to explore new experiences, fantasies, and activities together. This willingness can keep the sexual relationship exciting and fulfilling over time.

- **Avoiding Monotony:** Couples who are sexually compatible are less likely to fall into sexual routines that may lead to boredom and dissatisfaction.

**5. Adaptability:**

- **Adapting to Changes:** Sexual compatibility doesn't mean that partners have identical sexual preferences at all times. It also involves the ability to adapt and accommodate changes in desires or physical abilities over time.

### 6. Mutual Satisfaction:

- **Prioritizing Each Other's Satisfaction:** In sexually compatible relationships, both partners prioritize each other's sexual satisfaction. This mutual focus contributes to overall relationship satisfaction.

### 7. Prevention of Infidelity:

- **Reducing Temptations:** Sexual compatibility can reduce the temptation to seek sexual satisfaction outside the relationship. When both partners feel fulfilled within the relationship, the risk of infidelity is lower.

### 8. Seeking Professional Guidance:

- **Therapy and Counseling:** If sexual compatibility issues arise within a relationship, couples therapy or sex therapy can provide a safe and supportive environment for addressing these challenges.

It is important to note that sexual compatibility can evolve and change over time. Maintaining open communication and a willingness to adapt to each other's evolving desires and needs is essential for preserving sexual compatibility. Additionally, sexual compatibility should not be confused with physical appearance or attractiveness; it encompasses a broader spectrum of emotional, psychological, and physical elements that contribute to sexual satisfaction within a relationship.

# e) Sexual Dissatisfaction Issues and Their Contribution to Infidelity

Sexual dissatisfaction can be deeply distressing for men and can contribute to relationship challenges, including the risk of infidelity. While individual tolerance levels vary, there are several common sexual dissatisfaction issues that many men find difficult to tolerate. These unresolved sexual issues can strain relationships and create an environment where infidelity becomes more likely. Here are some sexual dissatisfaction issues and their potential impact on men:

### 1. Lack of Intimacy:

- **Issue:** A consistent lack of intimacy or emotional connection in the sexual relationship can lead to feelings of isolation and neglect.

- **Impact:** Men may feel emotionally unfulfilled and disconnected from their partners, which can erode the foundation of the relationship.

**2. Mismatched Libidos:**

- **Issue:** Mismatched libidos, where one partner desires sex more frequently than the other, can lead to frustration and dissatisfaction.
- **Impact:** The partner with a higher libido may feel unfulfilled and rejected, while the other may feel pressured or inadequate.

**3. Sexual Performance Anxiety:**

- **Issue:** Anxiety related to sexual performance, such as erectile dysfunction or premature ejaculation, can lead to feelings of inadequacy and frustration.
- **Impact:** Men experiencing performance anxiety may avoid sexual encounters, leading to decreased intimacy and connection.

**4. Unmet Fantasies and Desires:**

- **Issue:** Unmet sexual fantasies or desires can create feelings of longing and unfulfillment.
- **Impact:** If partners are not open to exploring these desires, men may feel unfulfilled and may seek out opportunities to fulfill these fantasies elsewhere.

**5. Emotional Neglect:**

- **Issue:** Emotional neglect within the relationship can extend to the sexual realm, leading to a lack of emotional connection during sex.
- **Impact:** Men may feel that sex is devoid of emotional intimacy and may seek it outside the relationship.

**6. Infrequent or Unsatisfying Sex:**

- **Issue:** Infrequent or unsatisfying sexual encounters can leave men feeling sexually unfulfilled.
- **Impact:** This dissatisfaction can lead to frustration and a desire for more frequent or satisfying sexual experiences, which can potentially be sought elsewhere.

**7. Communication Barriers:**

- **Issue:** Inability to communicate openly about sexual desires and preferences can lead to misunderstandings and unmet needs.
- **Impact:** Men may suppress their desires, leading to sexual frustration and a higher likelihood of seeking sexual satisfaction outside the relationship.

**8. Emotional Disconnect:**

- **Issue:** An overall emotional disconnect between partners can spill over into the bedroom, contributing to sexual dissatisfaction.

- **Impact:** Men may perceive sex as mechanical and devoid of emotional connection, making them more susceptible to infidelity.

It is important to note that unresolved sexual dissatisfaction issues can have a significant impact on relationship dynamics. Men who feel sexually unfulfilled may seek out new sexual experiences to satisfy their unmet needs or to escape the feelings of frustration and dissatisfaction. While infidelity is not the solution to these issues, it can appear as an attractive option when sexual needs are consistently unmet within the primary relationship.

Addressing sexual dissatisfaction issues through open communication, therapy, and a commitment to understanding and meeting each other's sexual needs is essential to maintaining a healthy and faithful relationship. Recognizing the signs of sexual dissatisfaction and addressing them proactively can help prevent the breakdown of trust and the temptation of infidelity.

# f) Communicating Openly About Sexual Desires

Effective communication about sexual desires is essential for building a fulfilling and satisfying sexual relationship. Open and honest discussions can lead to a better understanding of each other's needs, preferences, and boundaries. Here are examples of specific words, terms, or situations to address when communicating about sexual desires:

## 1. Preferred Activities:

- **Expressing Preferences:** Use clear and direct language to express your preferred sexual activities. For example, you might say, "I really enjoy when we try new positions," or "I love it when you initiate intimacy."

- **Fantasies:** Discuss sexual fantasies you'd like to explore and invite your partner to share theirs. Use phrases like, "I've had this fantasy about…"

## 2. Frequency and Timing:

- **Frequency:** Talk about how often you would like to engage in sexual activity. Be specific, such as saying, "I'd love to have sex at least three times a week."

- **Timing:** Discuss preferred times for sexual encounters that work for both partners. Consider factors like morning vs. evening or weekends vs. weekdays.

## 3. Emotional Connection:

- **Emotional Needs:** Address the importance of emotional connection during sex. You might say, "I feel most connected to you when we are emotionally present during sex."

- **Intimacy vs. Passion:** Distinguish between the desire for emotional intimacy and passionate encounters. For example, "Sometimes I crave deep emotional intimacy, while other times I want passionate, spontaneous sex."

## 4. Boundaries and Consent:

- **Limits and Boundaries:** Clearly define your sexual boundaries and limits. Use phrases like, "I'm not comfortable with that," or "Let us talk about our boundaries to ensure we both feel safe."

- **Consent:** Emphasize the importance of obtaining clear and enthusiastic consent before trying something new or engaging in any sexual activity.

## 5. Satisfaction and Feedback:

- **Expressing Satisfaction:** Share what makes you feel sexually satisfied and fulfilled. Use phrases like, "I love it when you do this; it really satisfies me."

- **Constructive Feedback:** Provide constructive feedback when necessary. Use a gentle approach, saying, "Can we try doing it this way next time? I think it would be even more enjoyable."

## 6. Communication Outside the Bedroom:

- **Non-Sexual Times:** Don't limit sexual discussions to the bedroom. Talk about your desires in non-sexual situations, such as over dinner or during a relaxing evening at home.

- **Check-Ins:** Periodically check in with each other about your sexual desires and whether they have evolved over time.

## 7. Respectful Language:

- **Use Respectful Language:** Ensure that the language you use is respectful and considerate of your partner's feelings. Avoid derogatory terms or language that may be offensive.

## 8. Emotional Connection:

- **Emphasize Emotional Connection:** Highlight the emotional connection and intimacy you want to experience during sexual encounters. Use phrases like, "I want us to feel emotionally connected when we make love."

## 9. Desire for Variety:

- **Desire for Novelty:** If you desire variety, express it openly. You might say, "I think it could be exciting to try new things in the bedroom from time to time."

## 10. Responsiveness:

- **Express Desire to Be Responsive:** Communicate your willingness to be responsive to your partner's desires and needs. For example, "I want to be attentive to what you enjoy."

Remember that open communication about sexual desires should be a two-way street. Encourage your partner to express their desires and actively listen to their needs as well. The goal is to create a safe and comfortable space for both partners to explore and fulfill each other's sexual desires while building a stronger and more satisfying sexual connection.

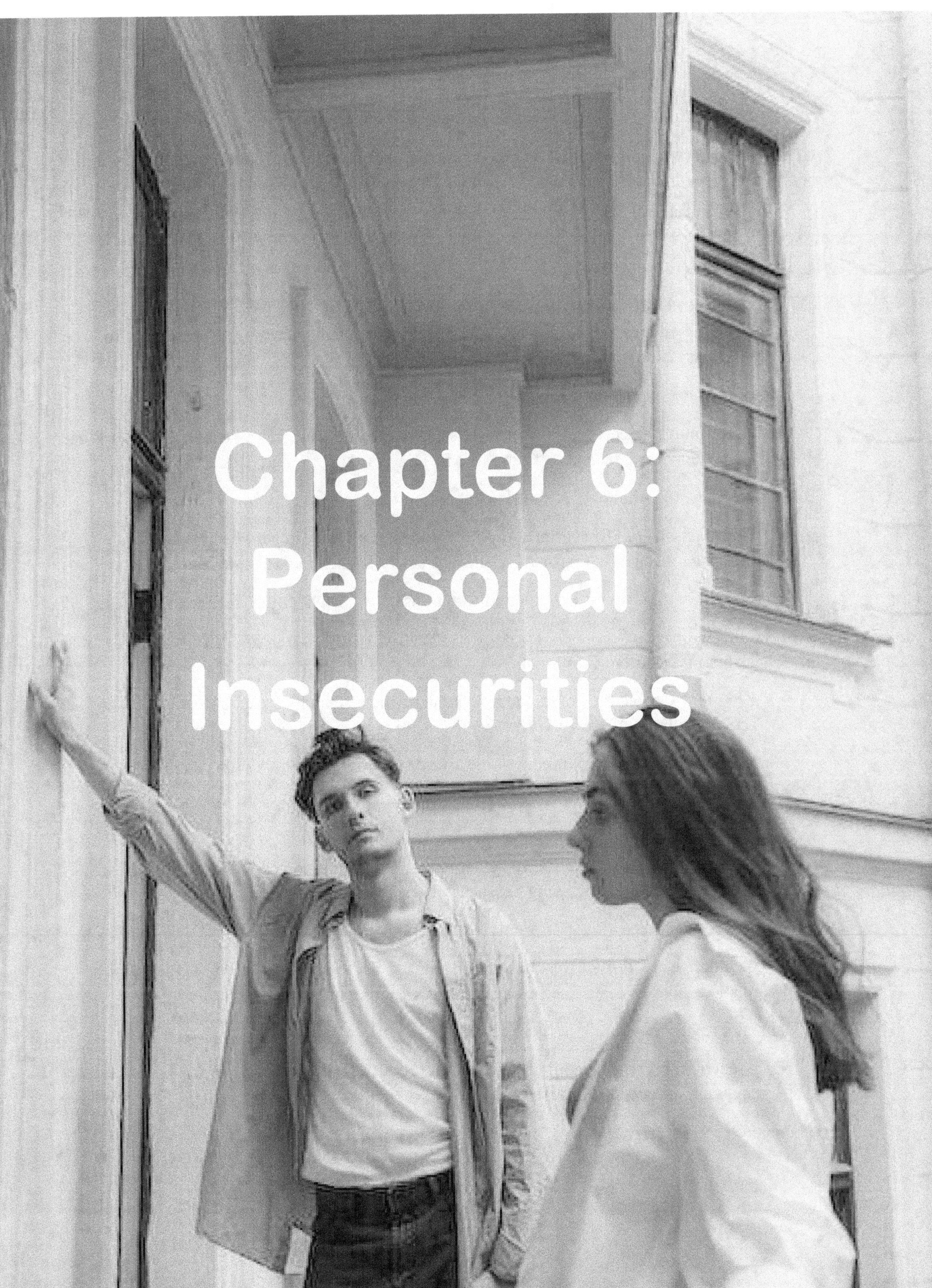

Chapter 6:
Personal
Insecurities

# a) Insecurity and Its Impact on Self-Esteem

Personal insecurities can significantly impact a man's self-esteem and contribute to vulnerability in the context of infidelity. While it is essential for both partners to build each other's self-esteem, there are inadvertent actions or situations a wife may create that could make her husband feel insecure. Here are some specific examples:

**1. Lack of Affection:**

- **Limited Physical Affection:** If a wife consistently withholds physical affection, such as hugs, kisses, or cuddling, her husband may feel unloved and unattractive, leading to insecurity about his desirability.

**2. Emotional Distance:**

- **Emotional Neglect:** Ignoring or dismissing a husband's emotional needs or concerns can create emotional distance, making him feel unimportant or undervalued.

**3. Comparisons to Others:**

- **Comparisons to Other Men:** Making frequent comparisons between the husband and other men, such as ex-partners, friends, or celebrities, can undermine his self-esteem.

- **Flirting with Others:** Engaging in flirtatious behavior with other men in the husband's presence can trigger jealousy and insecurity.

**4. Criticism and Negative Comments:**

- **Frequent Criticism:** Continuously criticizing the husband's appearance, choices, or actions without offering constructive feedback can erode his self-esteem.

- **Insensitive Remarks:** Making insensitive or hurtful remarks about his abilities or performance can damage his self-confidence.

**5. Lack of Validation:**

- **Failure to Acknowledge Accomplishments:** Neglecting to acknowledge the husband's achievements or downplaying his successes can lead to feelings of inadequacy.

**6. Unresolved Conflicts:**

- **Avoidance of Conflict Resolution:** Refusing to address or resolve conflicts within the relationship can create a sense of instability and insecurity.

**7. Broken Trust:**

- **Breach of Trust:** Engaging in actions that break trust, such as betraying confidences or engaging in deceptive behavior, can lead to insecurity.

**8. Inconsistent Support:**

- **Unreliable Support:** Being inconsistent in providing emotional support during challenging times can leave the husband feeling unsupported and insecure.

## 9. Disinterest in Intimacy:

- **Declining Intimacy:** Consistently declining sexual or emotional intimacy without explanation can make the husband feel undesirable and unloved.

## 10. Withholding Affection as Punishment:

- **Using Affection as a Weapon:** Using affection or intimacy as a tool for manipulation or punishment in the relationship can create emotional insecurity.

## 11. Unsolicited Advice:

- **Excessive Unsolicited Advice:** Continuously offering unsolicited advice or criticism about the husband's choices and decisions can make him question his abilities and judgment.

It is crucial to recognize that a healthy relationship is built on mutual respect, trust, and support. Addressing personal insecurities and fostering self-esteem requires open communication, empathy, and a commitment to building each other up. Both partners should work together to create an environment where both feel valued, loved, and secure in the relationship.

# b) Seeking Validation Outside the Relationship

Insecurity can lead some men to seek validation outside of their primary relationship. While it is important to remember that individuals are responsible for their choices, there are situations or actions by a wife that may unintentionally drive her husband to seek validation elsewhere. Here are specific examples:

## 1. Lack of Affirmation:

- **Failure to Express Affection:** If a wife rarely expresses affection, verbally or physically, her husband may seek affirmation from others who are more forthcoming with compliments and physical gestures.

## 2. Emotional Neglect:

- **Ignoring Emotional Needs:** If a wife consistently dismisses or ignores her husband's emotional needs or concerns, he may turn to someone who listens and validates his feelings.

## 3. Withholding Praise:

- **Failure to Acknowledge Achievements:** Not acknowledging or celebrating the husband's accomplishments or successes can make him feel unappreciated, leading him to seek praise elsewhere.

**4. Undermining Confidence:**

- **Consistent Criticism:** Habitually criticizing the husband's abilities, appearance, or choices can erode his self-confidence. Seeking validation from others may offer a temporary boost.

**5. Emotional Distance:**

- **Creating Emotional Distance:** Emotional distance or detachment within the relationship can lead the husband to seek emotional intimacy and validation from someone else.

**6. Comparisons to Others:**

- **Frequent Comparisons:** Continual comparisons between the husband and other men, highlighting perceived inadequacies, can lead him to seek validation from someone who appreciates him as he is.

**7. Refusing to Address Issues:**

- **Avoiding Conflict Resolution:** Refusing to address or resolve conflicts within the relationship may drive the husband to seek validation from someone who provides emotional support and listens to his concerns.

**8. Neglecting Intimacy:**

- **Declining Intimacy:** A consistent lack of physical or emotional intimacy within the relationship can leave the husband feeling undesired and may push him to seek validation elsewhere.

**9. Isolating Behavior:**

- **Isolation:** If a wife isolates her husband from his social circle or discourages him from maintaining friendships, he may seek validation from others who provide social connection.

**10. Unresolved Trust Issues:**

- **Breach of Trust:** Engaging in actions that break trust, such as betraying confidences or engaging in deceptive behavior, may drive the husband to seek validation from someone he perceives as more trustworthy.

**11. Using Affection as a Weapon:**

- **Using Affection as a Tool:** Using affection or intimacy as a tool for manipulation or punishment can push the husband to seek validation from someone who offers a more supportive and loving environment.

It is essential for both partners to actively address insecurities within the relationship through open communication, empathy, and a commitment to meeting each other's emotional needs. Seeking validation outside the relationship is not a healthy or productive way to address insecurity, and addressing the root causes of these insecurities within the relationship is crucial for maintaining trust and intimacy.

# c) Building Self-Confidence and Self-Worth

Building self-confidence and self-worth is essential for men to overcome personal insecurities and reduce the risk of infidelity. Here are specific examples of words, actions, and strategies that can help men enhance their self-confidence and self-worth:

## 1. Positive Self-Talk:

- **Affirmations:** Repeating positive affirmations daily, such as "I am confident and capable," can gradually shift one's self-perception.

## 2. Self-Acceptance:

- **Embrace Imperfections:** Understand that nobody is perfect, and it is okay to have flaws. Self-acceptance involves acknowledging imperfections and learning to love oneself regardless.

## 3. Setting Achievable Goals:

- **Small Steps:** Setting and achieving small, realistic goals can boost confidence. Each accomplishment contributes to a sense of competence and self-worth.

## 4. Self-Compassion:

- **Practice Self-Compassion:** Treat oneself with kindness and understanding, especially during times of perceived failure or mistakes.

## 5. Seeking Professional Help:

- **Therapy or Counseling:** Consider working with a therapist or counselor who specializes in self-esteem and self-worth issues. They can provide guidance and techniques to build self-confidence.

## 6. Surrounding Oneself with Supportive People:

- **Positive Relationships:** Maintain relationships with friends and family who uplift and support self-worth. Seek out people who appreciate and value you for who you are.

## 7. Celebrating Achievements:

- **Acknowledge Successes:** Celebrate achievements, no matter how small they may seem. Recognizing personal victories reinforces self-confidence.

## 8. Personal Development:

- **Continuous Learning:** Engage in lifelong learning and personal development activities. Acquiring new skills and knowledge can boost self-esteem.

## 9. Physical Health:

- **Exercise:** Regular physical activity can improve self-image and release endorphins, which contribute to a positive self-perception.

## 10. Self-Care:

- **Mental and Emotional Health:** Prioritize mental and emotional well-being through self-care practices like meditation, mindfulness, or journaling.

## 11. Facing Challenges:

- **Challenge Comfort Zones:** Actively seek out opportunities to step outside of one's comfort zone and confront fears or insecurities.

## 12. Seeking Feedback:

- **Ask for Constructive Feedback:** Seek feedback from trusted individuals who can provide constructive criticism and highlight areas of strength.

## 13. Mindfulness and Gratitude:

- **Practice Mindfulness:** Engage in mindfulness exercises to stay present and reduce self-doubt.

- **Gratitude Journal:** Keep a gratitude journal to remind oneself of positive aspects in life.

## 14. Personal Style and Grooming:

- **Self-Care in Appearance:** Taking care of one's physical appearance can positively impact self-confidence. Dressing well, grooming, and feeling comfortable in one's style can boost self-esteem.

## 15. Self-Reflection:

- **Regular Self-Reflection:** Spend time reflecting on one's values, strengths, and personal growth. Recognizing progress and personal development is essential for building self-worth.

Building self-confidence and self-worth is an ongoing process that involves self-awareness and self-compassion. It is important to be patient and kind to oneself throughout this journey. Additionally, seeking support from loved ones and professionals can provide valuable guidance and encouragement along the way.

Chapter 7:
Opportunity and
Temptation

# a) The Role of Opportunity in Infidelity

Opportunity plays a significant role in the occurrence of infidelity. While personal choices and relationship dynamics are crucial factors, the presence or absence of opportunities can influence the likelihood of cheating. Here is how opportunity can impact infidelity:

**1. Accessibility to Potential Partners:**

- **Social Circles:** If a man is frequently exposed to individuals who are open to extramarital affairs within his social or professional circles, the opportunity for infidelity increases.

- **Online Platforms:** The digital age has made it easier to connect with potential partners discreetly through dating apps, social media, or online communities, expanding the pool of available opportunities.

**2. Proximity and Convenience:**

- **Workplace Affairs:** Spending a significant amount of time with co-workers, especially during business trips or late nights at the office, can create proximity and opportunities for infidelity.

- **Proximity to Attractive Individuals:** Being in close proximity to someone they find attractive can increase temptation, particularly when there is privacy or secrecy involved.

**3. Emotional Vulnerability:**

- **Emotional Connection:** When a man is going through a period of emotional vulnerability or dissatisfaction within his primary relationship, he may be more susceptible to seeking emotional support and connection elsewhere.

- **Supportive Friends:** Supportive friends or acquaintances who offer a listening ear during difficult times can inadvertently become opportunities for emotional intimacy.

**4. Opportunity for Secrecy:**

- **Alone Time:** Having regular opportunities to be alone, whether due to work-related travel, personal hobbies, or other commitments, can create spaces for secretive interactions.

- **Cover Stories:** The ability to create cover stories or alibis for time spent with someone other than a spouse can make it easier to engage in an affair.

**5. Compartmentalization:**

- **Ability to Keep Affairs Separate:** Some men are adept at compartmentalizing their lives, which allows them to maintain separate relationships without their partners' knowledge.

**6. Lack of Accountability:**

- **Absence of Accountability:** When there is little or no accountability for one's actions, such as partners not checking each other's phone or social media accounts, it can facilitate secretive interactions.

## 7. Temptation and Opportunity Alignment:

- **Temptation Alignment:** The alignment of personal temptation with available opportunities can increase the likelihood of infidelity. When the desire for something new or different coincides with accessible options, the risk of cheating becomes higher.

## 8. Discretion and Secrecy:

- **Discreet Communication:** The ability to communicate discreetly, such as using encrypted messaging apps or secret email accounts, can enable secretive relationships.

## 9. Influence of Peer Behavior:

- **Peer Behavior:** If a man's friends or peers engage in or encourage extramarital affairs, it can normalize such behavior and create opportunities through introductions or shared experiences.

It is important to note that while opportunity can be a contributing factor, it does not excuse infidelity. Each individual is responsible for their choices and actions within a relationship. Recognizing the potential for opportunities and proactively addressing relationship issues, maintaining open communication, and reinforcing commitment can help reduce the temptation to cheat. Additionally, seeking support through counseling or therapy can assist couples in navigating challenges and maintaining fidelity.

# b) Recognizing and Avoiding Risky Situations

Recognizing and avoiding risky situations is crucial for maintaining fidelity and preventing infidelity. While it is impossible to completely eliminate all potential temptations, individuals and couples can take proactive steps to minimize the risk of infidelity. Here are specific examples, situations, and actions to help recognize and avoid risky situations:

## 1. Setting Boundaries:

- **Open Communication:** Have open and honest discussions with your partner about what constitutes appropriate behavior within your relationship. Define clear boundaries together.

## 2. Limiting Alone Time with Attractive Individuals:

- **Workplace Interaction:** Be mindful of spending excessive one-on-one time with attractive colleagues or acquaintances, especially outside of work hours.

- **Social Events:** When attending social events, try to avoid situations where you will be alone with someone who might be considered a temptation.

**3. Being Transparent:**

- **Share Plans:** Inform your partner about your plans, including social outings and meetings with friends or colleagues. Transparency can help build trust.

**4. Avoiding Private and Secretive Communication:**

- **Digital Boundaries:** Avoid engaging in private or secretive communication with individuals who may be seen as potential temptations. This includes avoiding secret chats, hidden messaging apps, or private email accounts.

**5. Managing Social Media:**

- **Social Media Boundaries:** Set boundaries on social media interactions, such as not accepting friend requests or private messages from individuals who may pose a temptation.

- **Refrain from Excessive Flirting:** Avoid engaging in flirtatious online conversations or interactions that could be misconstrued.

**6. Accountability:**

- **Accountability Partners:** Consider having a trusted friend or counselor who is aware of your commitment to your partner and can hold you accountable for your actions.

**7. Avoiding Isolation:**

- **Maintain Social Connections:** Stay engaged with your social circle and maintain friendships to reduce the risk of feeling isolated and seeking emotional connections elsewhere.

**8. Alcohol and Substance Use:**

- **Moderation:** Consume alcohol and other substances responsibly and in moderation, as impaired judgment can lead to risky behaviors.

**9. Recognizing Vulnerability:**

- **Self-Awareness:** Be aware of your emotional state and vulnerabilities. If you find yourself feeling emotionally vulnerable or dissatisfied, seek support from your partner or a counselor.

**10. Reinforcing Commitment:**

- **Revisit Commitment:** Periodically revisit your commitment to your partner and the values that underpin your relationship. Reminding yourself of your commitment can strengthen your resolve to avoid risky situations.

**11. Practicing Mindfulness:**

- **Mindfulness Techniques:** Practice mindfulness to stay present and make conscious choices in your interactions and relationships.

## 12. Seeking Professional Help:

- **Counseling or Therapy:** If you or your partner are concerned about infidelity or are facing challenges within your relationship, consider seeking the assistance of a qualified couples therapist or counselor.

Remember that avoiding risky situations is not about restricting your freedom or isolating yourself; it is about making conscious choices that prioritize your commitment to your partner and the health of your relationship. Open communication, trust, and mutual respect are essential foundations for building a strong and faithful partnership.

# c) Strengthening Trust and Boundaries in the Relationship

Strengthening trust and boundaries in a relationship is essential for preventing infidelity and creating a secure foundation. Trust is the cornerstone of a healthy partnership, and clear boundaries help both partners understand what is acceptable behavior within the relationship. Here are specific strategies to strengthen trust and boundaries:

## 1. Open and Honest Communication:

- **Regular Check-Ins:** Schedule regular check-in conversations where you discuss your feelings, needs, and concerns openly and honestly.

- **Share Vulnerabilities:** Encourage each other to share vulnerabilities and insecurities without fear of judgment.

## 2. Define Relationship Boundaries:

- **Mutual Understanding:** Establish mutual understanding of what constitutes acceptable and unacceptable behavior within the relationship.

- **Consent and Boundaries:** Ensure that both partners consent to and respect each other's boundaries.

## 3. Set Clear Expectations:

- **Discuss Expectations:** Have conversations about your expectations for the relationship, including commitments and fidelity.

- **Agree on Boundaries:** Reach agreements on specific boundaries related to friendships, communication with others, and interactions outside the relationship.

## 4. Build Emotional Intimacy:

- **Emotional Connection:** Invest time in building emotional intimacy by actively listening to each other, empathizing, and providing emotional support.

- **Foster Trust:** Emotional intimacy fosters trust, making it less likely for partners to seek emotional connections outside the relationship.

## 5. Establish Digital Boundaries:

- **Social Media Guidelines:** Discuss guidelines for social media interactions and privacy settings. Agree on what is appropriate to share online regarding your relationship.

- **Transparency:** Be transparent about your digital communication with others. Share passwords or openly discuss your online interactions when necessary.

## 6. Reinforce Commitment:

- **Remind Each Other:** Remind each other of your commitment and love for one another. Express your appreciation regularly.

- **Celebrate Milestones:** Celebrate relationship milestones and anniversaries as a way to reinforce your commitment.

## 7. Address Insecurities:

- **Support Each Other:** If either partner experiences insecurity or vulnerability, offer support and reassurance. Work together to address these feelings constructively.

## 8. Seek Professional Help:

- **Couples Therapy:** Consider couples therapy or counseling if trust issues or insecurities persist. A trained therapist can facilitate communication and provide strategies to rebuild trust.

## 9. Avoid Secrecy:

- **Transparency:** Avoid keeping secrets or engaging in secretive behavior. Transparency and honesty are key to trust-building.

## 10. Prioritize Quality Time:

- **Quality Time Together:** Prioritize quality time spent together, engaging in activities that strengthen your bond and connection.

## 11. Respect Privacy:

- **Respect Individual Privacy:** While maintaining transparency is important, also respect each other's individual privacy and personal space.

## 12. Consistent Effort:

- **Continuous Work:** Building and maintaining trust and boundaries is an ongoing process. It requires consistent effort from both partners.

## 13. Celebrate Achievements:

- **Acknowledge Growth:** Celebrate personal and relationship achievements, as well as the growth you experience together.

Strengthening trust and boundaries in a relationship is a collaborative effort that requires both partners to be committed to the well-being of their partnership. By fostering open communication, mutual respect, and a strong emotional connection, you can create a relationship that is resilient against the temptations and opportunities that may lead to infidelity.

PART III:
PREVENTION
AND HEALING

# Chapter 8: Communication and Trust

# a) The Foundation of a Healthy Relationship

A healthy relationship is built on a solid foundation of communication and trust. These two pillars are essential for maintaining a strong and lasting partnership. Here is a closer look at why they are the bedrock of a healthy relationship:

**1. Open and Honest Communication:**

- **Trust Building:** Communication is the primary means through which trust is established and maintained. When partners communicate openly and honestly, they demonstrate that they can rely on each other for truth and transparency.

- **Conflict Resolution:** Effective communication allows couples to address conflicts and disagreements constructively. It enables them to express their feelings, needs, and concerns in a way that fosters understanding and compromise.

- **Emotional Connection:** Sharing thoughts, dreams, and emotions through communication strengthens the emotional connection between partners. It allows them to feel seen, heard, and valued.

- **Intimacy:** Communication is not just about verbal exchange but also includes non-verbal cues, such as physical affection and gestures of love. These forms of communication foster intimacy and closeness.

**2. Trust and Reliability:**

- **Consistency:** Trust is built on the consistency of one's actions over time. Partners who consistently demonstrate reliability, honesty, and integrity earn each other's trust.

- **Predictability:** Trust is also about predictability. In a healthy relationship, partners can predict each other's behavior based on their history of trustworthiness.

- **Vulnerability:** Trust allows partners to be vulnerable with each other, sharing their fears, insecurities, and dreams without fear of judgment or betrayal.

**3. Respect and Support:**

- **Mutual Respect:** Healthy communication and trust are rooted in mutual respect. Partners respect each other's boundaries, opinions, and individuality.

- **Supportive Environment:** In a trusting relationship, partners create a supportive environment where they can rely on each other for emotional and practical support.

**4. Emotional Safety:**

- **Emotional Safety:** A healthy relationship provides emotional safety, where partners can express their feelings without fear of ridicule or dismissal.

- **Shared Goals:** Trust and communication enable partners to collaborate on shared goals and aspirations, whether they are related to family, career, or personal growth.

**5. Growth and Adaptation:**

- **Adaptation:** Partners who communicate openly and trust each other can adapt to changing circumstances and challenges together. They are more resilient in the face of adversity.

- **Personal Growth:** A healthy relationship encourages personal growth and self-improvement. Partners support each other's goals and aspirations, fostering growth as individuals and as a couple.

**6. Conflict Resolution:**

- **Conflict Management:** Trust and communication are crucial for effective conflict resolution. In a healthy relationship, conflicts are seen as opportunities for growth and understanding, not as threats.

- **Forgiveness:** Trust allows for forgiveness when mistakes are made. Partners who trust each other are more likely to forgive and work towards resolution rather than holding grudges.

A relationship without open and honest communication and trust is like a house built on a shaky foundation—it is vulnerable to crumbling under pressure. In contrast, a relationship grounded in these principles is more likely to withstand the challenges that life throws its way. Cultivating these qualities requires effort, patience, and a commitment from both partners, but the rewards of a strong, healthy relationship are immeasurable.

# b) Effective Communication Strategies

Effective communication is the cornerstone of a healthy and thriving relationship. It is a skill that can be learned and honed over time. Here are some effective communication strategies to strengthen your relationship:

**1. Active Listening:**

- **Be Fully Present:** When your partner is speaking, give them your full attention. Put away distractions, make eye contact, and show that you are actively listening.

- **Reflective Responses:** After your partner speaks, reflect back what you have heard to ensure you understand correctly. For example, "I hear you saying that you felt hurt when…"

**2. Use "I" Statements:**

- **Express Feelings:** Use "I" statements to express your feelings and needs rather than making accusatory or blaming statements. For example, "I feel hurt when…"

- **Avoid "You" Blaming:** Instead of saying, "You always do this," say, "I feel frustrated when this happens."

### 3. Empathize:

- **Understand Emotions:** Try to understand your partner's emotions and point of view. Show empathy by acknowledging their feelings. For example, "I can see why you might feel that way."

- **Validation:** Validate your partner's feelings even if you don't agree with their perspective. Validation can help them feel heard and respected.

### 4. Avoid Defensiveness:

- **Stay Open-Minded:** Avoid becoming defensive when your partner expresses concerns or criticism. Instead, remain open to their viewpoint and be willing to discuss it.

- **Seek Clarification:** If you don't understand something, ask for clarification rather than making assumptions.

### 5. Non-Verbal Communication:

- **Body Language:** Pay attention to your body language and non-verbal cues. Maintain open and non-threatening posture. Avoid eye-rolling or dismissive gestures.

### 6. Timing Matters:

- **Choose the Right Time:** Timing is crucial in communication. Avoid addressing sensitive issues when one or both of you are stressed, tired, or in a rush.

- **Schedule Conversations:** If necessary, schedule important discussions when you both have time and energy to focus on them.

### 7. Stay Calm:

- **Manage Emotions:** Practice emotional self-regulation. If a conversation becomes heated, take a break to cool off before continuing.

- **Use "Timeouts":** Agree on a signal or word that indicates a need for a timeout when emotions escalate. This allows both partners to step away and regroup.

### 8. Problem-Solving:

- **Collaborate:** Approach conflicts as problems to be solved together, rather than battles to be won. Work as a team to find solutions that satisfy both of your needs.

- **Compromise:** Be willing to compromise and find middle ground when disagreements arise.

### 9. Be Clear and Specific:

- **Use Clear Language:** Avoid vague or ambiguous language. Be specific about your needs, concerns, and expectations.

- **Ask for What You Want:** If you want something, ask for it directly rather than hoping your partner will guess.

## 10. Express Appreciation:

- **Gratitude:** Regularly express gratitude and appreciation for your partner. Acknowledge their efforts and contributions to the relationship.

## 11. Seek Professional Help:

- **Counseling:** If communication challenges persist, consider seeking the help of a couples' counselor or therapist who can provide guidance and mediation.

Effective communication is a dynamic skill that requires ongoing effort and practice. By using these strategies, you can create a more open, respectful, and understanding environment within your relationship, which strengthens trust and deepens your connection.

# c) Rebuilding Trust After Infidelity

Rebuilding trust after infidelity is a challenging but possible journey for couples who are committed to healing their relationship. While there is no one-size-fits-all solution, here are steps and strategies to help rebuild trust:

## 1. Open and Honest Communication:

- **Acknowledgment of Betrayal:** The partner who cheated should acknowledge their actions, take responsibility for the betrayal, and express genuine remorse.

- **Transparency:** Commit to complete transparency in all aspects of the relationship, including digital communication and social media.

- **Reveal Motivations:** The cheater should openly discuss the motivations and circumstances that led to the infidelity. Understanding the root causes is essential for preventing future occurrences.

## 2. Seek Professional Help:

- **Couples Counseling:** Consider seeking the assistance of a qualified couples therapist or counselor who specializes in infidelity. A therapist can facilitate difficult conversations and provide guidance.

- **Individual Therapy:** Both partners may benefit from individual therapy to address personal issues and emotions related to the infidelity.

## 3. Establish Boundaries:

- **Revisit Relationship Boundaries:** Both partners should revisit and clearly define their relationship boundaries, ensuring that they are aligned with both partners' needs and expectations.

- **Agree on Boundaries:** Reach new agreements on boundaries to help prevent future breaches of trust.

### 4. Consistency Over Time:

- **Demonstrate Trustworthiness:** The partner who cheated should demonstrate consistent trustworthiness over time. Actions should align with words to rebuild credibility.

- **Patience:** Rebuilding trust is a gradual process, and it may take time for the hurt partner to feel secure again.

### 5. Forgiveness and Healing:

- **Emotional Healing:** The hurt partner should allow themselves time and space to process their emotions, including anger, hurt, and betrayal.

- **Work on Forgiveness:** Forgiveness is a choice and a process. The hurt partner should work towards forgiving their partner if they believe it is possible and in the best interest of the relationship.

### 6. Reconnect Emotionally:

- **Rekindle Emotional Intimacy:** Focus on rekindling emotional intimacy and connection through deep conversations, shared experiences, and quality time together.

- **Rebuilding Friendship:** Rebuild the foundation of friendship within the relationship. A strong friendship can provide a sense of security and trust.

### 7. Accountability:

- **Accept Accountability:** The partner who cheated should accept accountability for their actions and be willing to discuss any lingering doubts or concerns from the hurt partner.

- **Regular Check-Ins:** Schedule regular check-in conversations to gauge progress and address any lingering issues.

### 8. Avoid Defensiveness:

- **Openness to Feedback:** Both partners should remain open to feedback and avoid becoming defensive during discussions related to the infidelity.

### 9. Rebuild Shared Goals:

- **Revisit Relationship Goals:** Discuss and revisit your shared goals, dreams, and aspirations as a couple to reestablish a sense of direction.

### 10. Patience and Understanding:

- **Be Patient:** Understand that healing takes time and may involve setbacks. Be patient with each other and yourselves.

## 11. Monitor Triggers:

- **Identify Triggers:** Recognize potential triggers that may evoke negative emotions or memories related to the infidelity. Work together to manage these triggers.

Rebuilding trust after infidelity is a complex process that requires mutual effort, understanding, and a commitment to change and growth. It is important to remember that not all relationships can fully recover from infidelity, and some may ultimately choose to separate. However, for couples who are willing to invest in rebuilding trust, it is possible to create a stronger, more resilient relationship than before, built on a foundation of open communication, transparency, and mutual respect.

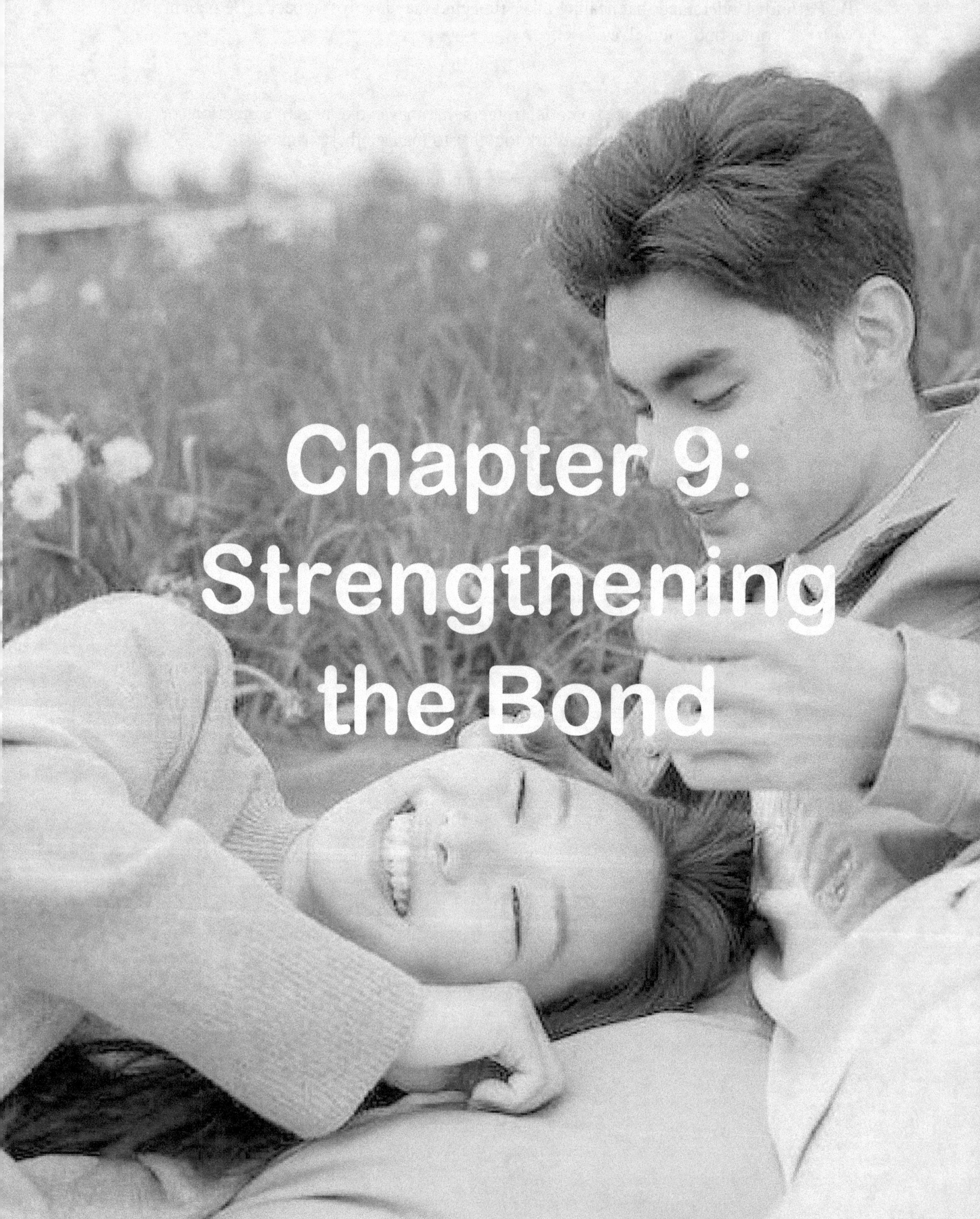

# Chapter 9: Strengthening the Bond

# a) Rekindling Romance and Passion

Rekindling romance and passion in a relationship is a powerful way to prevent cheating and heal a troubled partnership. When couples prioritize and nurture their romantic connection, they are less likely to seek fulfillment outside the relationship. Here are strategies to help you rekindle romance and passion:

**1. Quality Time:**

- **Date Nights:** Schedule regular date nights or special outings to focus on each other without distractions.

- **Quality Over Quantity:** It is not just about spending time together; it is about making the time meaningful and memorable.

**2. Spontaneity:**

- **Surprises:** Surprise your partner with small gestures, gifts, or acts of kindness to keep the relationship exciting.

- **Spur-of-the-Moment Adventures:** Occasionally, plan spontaneous adventures or surprises that break the routine.

**3. Physical Intimacy:**

- **Physical Affection:** Prioritize physical intimacy through hugging, cuddling, kissing, and holding hands regularly.

- **Variety in Intimacy:** Explore new ways to be intimate and adventurous in the bedroom to maintain a healthy sex life.

**4. Communication:**

- **Express Desire:** Communicate your desires and fantasies to your partner in a loving and open way.

- **Listen Actively:** Be attentive when your partner shares their desires, and actively work together to fulfill each other's needs.

**5. Emotional Connection:**

- **Deep Conversations:** Engage in deep, meaningful conversations that go beyond daily routines and delve into your thoughts, dreams, and aspirations.

- **Active Listening:** Show genuine interest in your partner's feelings and concerns, and listen actively without judgment.

### 6. Recreate Memories:

- **Revisit Special Places:** Take trips to places that hold sentimental value for your relationship to reminisce and create new memories.

- **Anniversaries and Milestones:** Celebrate anniversaries and other relationship milestones with special activities or rituals.

### 7. Affectionate Gestures:

- **Love Notes:** Leave love notes or send affectionate texts to remind your partner of your love.

- **Small Acts of Kindness:** Perform small acts of kindness, like making breakfast in bed or doing chores for your partner, to show appreciation.

### 8. Shared Interests:

- **Explore Hobbies:** Discover new hobbies or interests that you can pursue together, fostering a sense of adventure and shared enjoyment.

### 9. Compliments and Appreciation:

- **Express Love:** Compliment your partner and express your love and appreciation regularly.

### 10. Surprise Getaways:

- **Weekend Escapes:** Plan surprise weekend getaways to rejuvenate your connection and create lasting memories.

### 11. Reliving Firsts:

- **First Date Recreations:** Recreate your first date or early relationship experiences to relive the excitement of your early days together.

### 12. Time Apart:

- **Individual Space:** Allow each other space for personal growth and independence, which can make time spent together more meaningful.

### 13. Seek Help When Needed:

- **Counseling:** If you find that your relationship struggles to rekindle romance and passion despite efforts, consider seeking the guidance of a couples therapist or counselor.

Remember that rekindling romance and passion is an ongoing process that requires effort and creativity from both partners. By consistently investing in your relationship's emotional and physical connection, you can strengthen your bond and make your partnership resilient against the temptation of infidelity.

# b) Activities to Foster Connection and Intimacy

Engaging in activities that foster connection and intimacy is a wonderful way to strengthen your bond and prevent cheating. These activities create opportunities for quality time together and help you deepen your emotional and physical connection. Here are various activities to consider:

**1. Couple's Retreat:**

- **Escape Together:** Plan a romantic couple's retreat to a peaceful destination where you can relax, reconnect, and enjoy each other's company without distractions.

**2. Outdoor Adventures:**

- **Hiking:** Go on a hike or nature walk together, allowing you to connect with each other and with the beauty of the outdoors.

- **Camping:** Spend a weekend camping, where you can build a campfire, cook meals together, and stargaze.

- **Kayaking or Canoeing:** Explore a calm river or lake by kayaking or canoeing as a team-building experience.

**3. Cooking Together:**

- **Cooking Classes:** Enroll in cooking classes as a couple, and learn to prepare new dishes together.

- **Home-Cooked Meals:** Cook a special meal at home, from appetizers to dessert, and enjoy a candlelit dinner.

**4. Dancing:**

- **Dance Classes:** Take dance classes together, whether it is ballroom, salsa, or swing dancing.

- **Dance Nights:** Go out for a night of dancing at a local club or event.

**5. Arts and Culture:**

- **Museum Visits:** Explore museums, art galleries, or cultural exhibits, discussing your impressions and interpretations.

- **Theater or Live Performances:** Attend live theater shows, concerts, or performances to enjoy art and culture together.

**6. Volunteer Together:**

- **Community Service:** Participate in volunteer activities or charity events as a team, strengthening your bond through shared values.

**7. Travel Adventures:**

- **Road Trips:** Embark on spontaneous road trips or planned vacations to explore new places and create lasting memories.

- **Travel Journal:** Keep a travel journal together, documenting your experiences and reflections.

## 8. Creative Pursuits:

- **Art and Craft Projects:** Collaborate on art or craft projects, such as painting, pottery, or DIY home decor.

- **Writing or Journaling:** Write love letters, poems, or journal entries to express your feelings and thoughts.

## 9. Wellness Activities:

- **Yoga or Meditation:** Practice yoga or meditation together to promote relaxation and emotional connection.

- **Couples Massage:** Enjoy a couples' massage session to unwind and connect through touch.

Remember that the key to these activities is to enjoy them together and use them as opportunities to communicate, laugh, and build shared experiences. By actively participating in these bonding activities, you will nurture your emotional and physical connection, making your relationship more resilient and fulfilling.

# c) Reinventing the Relationship

Sometimes, reinventing the relationship is necessary to prevent cheating or heal after infidelity. This process involves reevaluating and reshaping the dynamics, expectations, and overall structure of the partnership. Here are steps to consider when reinventing your relationship:

## 1. Reflect on Your Relationship:

- **Individual Reflection:** Each partner should take time to reflect on their feelings, needs, and desires within the relationship.

- **Shared Reflection:** Share your reflections and insights with each other in an open and non-judgmental way.

## 2. Redefine Your Goals:

- **Clarify Expectations:** Discuss and clarify your expectations for the relationship, addressing any gaps or misalignments.

- **Set New Goals:** Reevaluate your shared goals and aspirations, and adjust them to reflect your current desires and circumstances.

## 3. Relationship Reinvention Discussion:

- **Honest Conversations:** Engage in honest and open conversations about the future of your relationship, considering what changes are necessary.
- **Mutual Consent:** Reinventing the relationship should be a mutual decision, with both partners actively participating in the process.

## 4. Seek Guidance:

- **Professional Help:** Consider working with a couples therapist or counselor who specializes in relationship reinvention. They can provide guidance and facilitate these conversations.

## 5. Embrace Change:

- **Accept Growth:** Understand that growth and change are natural parts of any long-term relationship. Embrace these changes as opportunities for renewal.

## 6. Rebuilding Trust:

- **Rebuild Trust:** If the relationship has been impacted by infidelity, prioritize rebuilding trust through communication, transparency, and accountability.

## 7. Create a Shared Vision:

- **Shared Vision:** Collaboratively create a shared vision for your future together, outlining the kind of relationship you both want.
- **Mutual Goals:** Identify mutual goals and strategies to achieve them.

## 8. Reinvent Intimacy:

- **Rediscover Intimacy:** Explore new ways to be intimate emotionally and physically. Be open to trying new things in the bedroom and experimenting with your emotional connection.

## 9. Establish New Routines:

- **Create New Traditions:** Establish new routines and traditions that bring excitement and freshness to your daily life.

Remember that reinventing the relationship is an ongoing process, and it may take time to fully realize the changes you desire. Be patient with yourselves and each other as you work together to redefine and strengthen your partnership. It is an opportunity for growth, renewal, and a deeper connection that can help prevent cheating and promote a healthy, fulfilling relationship.

# Chapter 10: Seeking Professional Help

# a) The Benefits of Couples Therapy

Couples therapy, also known as marriage or relationship counseling, offers numerous benefits for couples facing challenges related to infidelity, trust issues, or any other relationship struggles. Here are the key benefits of couples therapy:

**1. Improved Communication:**

- **Effective Communication:** Couples therapy provides a structured and safe environment for partners to learn and practice healthy communication skills. They can express their thoughts, feelings, and concerns more openly and constructively.

- **Conflict Resolution:** Therapists teach couples conflict resolution techniques, helping them navigate disagreements and conflicts with greater understanding and empathy.

**2. Enhanced Understanding:**

- **Insight into Each Other:** Therapy sessions facilitate a deeper understanding of each other's perspectives, needs, and emotions. This insight can lead to increased empathy and compassion.

- **Identifying Patterns:** Therapists help couples identify negative patterns of interaction and behavior, enabling them to make positive changes.

**3. Rebuilding Trust:**

- **Trust Repair:** For couples dealing with infidelity, therapy offers a structured framework for rebuilding trust. Therapists guide discussions around the betrayal, accountability, and transparency.

- **Accountability:** Therapists help the partner who cheated take responsibility for their actions and demonstrate commitment to rebuilding trust.

**4. Conflict Resolution:**

- **Conflict Management:** Therapy equips couples with effective conflict management skills, reducing the intensity and frequency of arguments.

- **Fair Fighting:** Therapists teach couples how to engage in "fair fighting," where conflicts are addressed constructively without harm to the relationship.

**5. Emotional Expression:**

- **Emotional Release:** Couples therapy provides a safe space for partners to express their emotions and vulnerabilities, fostering emotional intimacy.

- **Validation:** Therapists validate each partner's feelings and experiences, helping them feel heard and understood.

**6. Strengthening the Relationship:**

- **Improving Relationship Satisfaction:** Couples therapy can significantly improve relationship satisfaction, leading to a more fulfilling partnership.

- **Deepening Connection:** Through therapy, couples often develop a deeper emotional connection and a stronger bond.

## 7. Learning New Skills:

- **Communication Skills:** Therapy equips couples with practical skills they can use to maintain a healthy relationship beyond the therapy sessions.

- **Problem-Solving:** Couples learn problem-solving techniques that help them address challenges more effectively.

## 8. Prevention and Preparedness:

- **Cheating Prevention:** Couples therapy can serve as a preventative measure by addressing underlying issues and vulnerabilities that may lead to infidelity.

- **Preparedness:** Couples learn how to identify potential stressors and challenges, enabling them to address issues before they escalate.

## 9. Objective Perspective:

- **Neutral Mediation:** Therapists act as neutral mediators who can offer an objective perspective on the relationship, helping partners gain clarity on their issues.

## 10. Post-Infidelity Healing:

- Recovery Process: For couples dealing with infidelity, therapy guides them through the healing process, helping them decide whether they can move forward together or separately.

## 11. Personal Growth:

- Individual Growth: Couples therapy also encourages individual growth and self-awareness, which can benefit both partners in various aspects of their lives.

## 12. Long-Term Success:

- Sustainability: The skills and insights gained in therapy can contribute to the long-term success and resilience of the relationship.

Couples therapy is a valuable resource for couples seeking to address their relationship challenges, whether they are dealing with infidelity, trust issues, communication problems, or other concerns. It provides a structured, supportive, and confidential space for partners to work collaboratively towards a healthier, more fulfilling relationship.

# b) Finding the Right Therapist

Finding the right therapist is a crucial step in your journey to healing and strengthening your relationship. Here is a detailed guide on how to find the therapist who is the best fit for you and your partner:

**1. Determine Your Needs:**

- Before you start searching, take some time to identify your specific needs and goals for therapy. What issues are you facing? Do you have any preferences regarding the therapist's gender, approach, or expertise? Knowing your needs will help you narrow down your options.

**2. Research Therapists:**

- Start by conducting research online. You can use search engines, therapist directories, or referral websites to find potential therapists in your area. Ask for recommendations from friends, family, or your primary care physician.

**3. Check Credentials:**

- Verify that the therapist is licensed and accredited in your state or country. Check their qualifications, including their educational background and any specialized training in couples therapy or relationship counseling.

**4. Read Reviews and Testimonials:**

- Look for online reviews and testimonials from previous clients. While these can be helpful, remember that individual experiences may vary, so consider them as one factor in your decision.

**5. Interview Potential Therapists:**

- Contact the therapists you are interested in and schedule initial consultations or interviews. Many therapists offer free or low-cost initial sessions to discuss your concerns and assess whether they are a good fit for you.

**6. Ask Questions:**

- Prepare a list of questions to ask potential therapists during the interviews. Some questions to consider include:

- What is your approach to couples therapy?

- How do you handle issues related to infidelity and trust?

- What is your availability, including session times and location?

- How do you structure your sessions, and what is the expected duration of therapy?

- What are your fees, insurance policies, and payment options?

- Can you provide references from past clients?

**7. Assess Compatibility:**

- Pay attention to how you feel during the interview. Do you feel comfortable and heard? Assess whether you and your partner feel a connection with the therapist. Trust your instincts; a good therapeutic relationship is built on trust and rapport.

**8. Specialized Expertise:**

- If you are dealing with specific issues, such as infidelity, trust issues, or sexual concerns, consider therapists who specialize in these areas. They may have the expertise and experience to address your unique challenges.

**9. Inquire About Approach:**

- Discuss the therapist's approach to couples therapy. Some therapists use techniques like cognitive-behavioral therapy, while others may focus on emotionally focused therapy or other modalities. Choose an approach that aligns with your goals and preferences.

**10. Consider Logistics:** - Take into account practical factors such as the therapist's location, office hours, and the convenience of session times. Ensure that the logistics fit with your schedule and lifestyle.

**11. Evaluate Costs:** - Understand the therapist's fees, insurance coverage, and payment options. Couples therapy can be an investment in your relationship, so clarify the financial aspects upfront.

**12. Trust Your Gut:** - Ultimately, trust your intuition when making a decision. The right therapist for you is one with whom you and your partner feel comfortable, understood, and supported.

**13. Discuss Expectations:** - Once you have chosen a therapist, have an open discussion about your expectations and goals for therapy. Establish clear boundaries, responsibilities, and communication channels for both you and your therapist.

Remember that finding the right therapist may take some time and effort, but it is a crucial step in the healing process. A skilled and compassionate therapist can provide you and your partner with the guidance and support needed to address your relationship challenges and work towards a healthier, more fulfilling partnership.

## c) Navigating the Healing Process

Navigating the healing process through couples therapy is a journey that requires commitment, effort, and patience. Here is a guide to help you understand what to expect and how to make the most of your therapy experience:

**1. Commit to the Process:**

- Understand that healing and rebuilding trust in your relationship takes time. Commit to attending therapy sessions regularly and being actively engaged in the process.

**2. Set Realistic Expectations:**

- Be realistic about what therapy can achieve. It won't magically solve all your problems overnight, but it can provide the tools and support needed to work through challenges.

**3. Be Open and Honest:**

- In therapy, honesty is key. Be open about your thoughts, feelings, and concerns. Avoid holding back, as this can hinder progress.

**4. Address Infidelity and Trust Issues:**

- If infidelity is a part of your relationship struggles, be prepared to address it directly. Therapy provides a safe space to discuss the betrayal, its impact, and the steps needed to rebuild trust.

**5. Communication Skills:**

- Work with your therapist to improve your communication skills. Learn how to express yourself effectively and listen actively to your partner.

**6. Conflict Resolution:**

- Therapy can help you develop healthier ways to resolve conflicts. Practice these techniques both in and outside of therapy sessions.

**7. Individual and Joint Work:**

- Therapy may involve individual sessions in addition to joint sessions with your partner. Use these individual sessions for self-reflection and personal growth.

**8. Homework Assignments:**

- Expect homework assignments from your therapist. These tasks are designed to reinforce what you have learned in therapy and apply it to real-life situations.

**9. Embrace Vulnerability:**

- Embrace vulnerability as part of the healing process. Share your feelings, fears, and insecurities with your partner and therapist.

**10. Patience and Understanding:** - Understand that healing is not linear. There will be ups and downs along the way. Patience and empathy for both yourself and your partner are essential.

**11. Active Participation:** - Be an active participant in your therapy. Ask questions, seek clarification, and provide feedback to your therapist.

**12. Set Goals:** - Work with your therapist to set clear goals for your relationship. These goals should be specific, measurable, and achievable.

**13. Self-Care:** - Prioritize self-care for both yourself and your partner. Take care of your physical and emotional well-being, as it will benefit your relationship.

**14. Communication Outside of Therapy:** - Practice the communication skills you learn in therapy during your daily interactions with your partner. Consistent application is key to lasting change.

**15. Evaluate Progress:** - Periodically assess your progress with your therapist. Discuss whether your goals are being met and make adjustments as needed.

**16. Seek Support:** - Reach out to a support network of friends or family who can provide encouragement and understanding during this challenging time.

**17. Be Open to Change:** - Be open to change and growth, both individually and as a couple. Understand that the healing process may lead to a transformed and stronger relationship.

**18. Know When to Seek Additional Help:** - If you feel that therapy is not producing the desired results or if you encounter significant roadblocks, consider discussing alternative therapeutic approaches or seeking a second opinion.

**19. Celebrate Progress:** - Celebrate your achievements along the way, no matter how small they may seem. Acknowledge and appreciate the effort you and your partner are putting into healing and strengthening your relationship.

Remember that every couple's journey through therapy is unique. While it may be challenging at times, therapy offers the potential for growth, healing, and the restoration of trust in your relationship. With dedication and a willingness to work together, you can navigate the healing process and build a healthier and more resilient partnership.

Chapter 11:
Moving Forward

Moving forward after infidelity is a significant step in the healing process. Forgiveness and letting go of the past are integral to rebuilding trust and creating a healthier future for your relationship. Here is a guide on how to navigate forgiveness and the process of letting go:

**1. Understand Forgiveness:**

- Recognize that forgiveness is a choice, not a mandate. It is a conscious decision to release feelings of anger, resentment, and the desire for revenge.

**2. Embrace Healing:**

- Understand that forgiveness is a part of the healing process for both you and your partner. It can lead to emotional relief and personal growth.

**3. Self-Compassion:**

- Begin by showing yourself self-compassion. Acknowledge your own pain, hurt, and emotions related to the infidelity.

**4. Process Your Emotions:**

- Allow yourself to feel the full range of emotions associated with the betrayal, including anger, sadness, and grief. These emotions are valid and need to be acknowledged and processed.

**5. Communication:**

- Engage in open and honest communication with your partner about your feelings and the process of forgiveness. Share your struggles, fears, and hopes.

**6. Seek Support:**

- Consider seeking support from a therapist or counselor who specializes in infidelity and healing. They can provide guidance and a safe space to explore your emotions.

**7. Identify the Motivations:**

- Understand the motivations and circumstances that led to the infidelity. This can provide insight into the root causes and help prevent a recurrence.

**8. Empathy and Understanding:**

- Develop empathy and understanding for your partner's perspective and struggles. This doesn't mean condoning the behavior but recognizing that humans are fallible.

**9. Set Boundaries:**

- Establish clear boundaries for your relationship moving forward. These boundaries should address behaviors and actions that are unacceptable.

**10. Take Your Time:** - Forgiveness is a process, and it may take time. Don't rush yourself into forgiving if you are not ready. Healing occurs at different paces for everyone.

**11. Practice Self-Care:** - Prioritize self-care, including physical and emotional well-being. Take care of yourself as you navigate this challenging terrain.

**12. Reflect on the Relationship:** - Reflect on the overall health of your relationship. Consider the positive aspects and the reasons you want to work toward forgiveness and healing.

**13. Accept Imperfections:** - Accept that both you and your partner are imperfect. Forgiveness involves recognizing that people make mistakes, and it is possible to move past them.

**14. Release the Grudge:** - Let go of the grudge or desire for revenge. Holding onto these feelings can hinder your own emotional well-being.

**15. Rebuilding Trust:** - Understand that forgiveness is not the same as blindly trusting again. Trust is rebuilt over time through consistent actions and transparency.

**16. Reconnect Emotionally:** - Focus on rebuilding emotional intimacy and connection within your relationship. Share your dreams, goals, and desires as a way to bond.

**17. Monitor Progress:** - Periodically evaluate your progress in the forgiveness process. Celebrate milestones and recognize your growth.

**18. Give It Time:** - Recognize that forgiveness may come in stages. It is okay if it takes time to fully forgive and let go.

**19. A New Beginning:** - Consider this phase as a new beginning for your relationship. Use the lessons learned from the past to build a stronger, more resilient partnership.

Remember that forgiveness is a personal journey, and it is okay to seek professional help or support from loved ones along the way. It is a transformative process that can lead to greater emotional freedom, healing, and the possibility of a renewed and healthier relationship.

## b) Rebuilding a Stronger Relationship

Moving forward after infidelity requires intentional effort to rebuild a stronger and more resilient relationship. Here are steps to help you and your partner navigate this process:

**1. Open Communication:**

- Continue open and honest communication with your partner. Share your thoughts, feelings, and concerns, fostering a deeper connection.

**2. Transparency:**

- Emphasize transparency and honesty in all aspects of your relationship. Be accountable for your actions and decisions.

### 3. Rebuilding Trust:

- Understand that trust takes time to rebuild. Consistently demonstrate trustworthiness through your actions.

### 4. Seek Professional Help:

- Consider ongoing couples therapy to address underlying issues, improve communication, and prevent future problems.

### 5. Address Underlying Issues:

- Work together to identify and address the root causes of the infidelity, whether they relate to emotional disconnection, dissatisfaction, or personal insecurities.

### 6. Set New Boundaries:

- Establish clear boundaries in your relationship that promote trust and prevent future infidelity. Discuss what behaviors are unacceptable.

### 7. Forgiveness:

- Continue to work on forgiveness, both for yourself and your partner. Forgiveness is a process that may take time.

### 8. Reconnect Emotionally:

- Focus on rebuilding emotional intimacy. Spend quality time together, engage in deep conversations, and express your love and appreciation regularly.

### 9. Reinvent Your Relationship:

- Consider this phase as an opportunity to reinvent your relationship. Rediscover shared interests, set new goals, and create a fresh vision for your future together.

**10. Prioritize Self-Care:** - Continue to prioritize self-care for both yourself and your partner. Emotional well-being is essential for a healthy relationship.

**11. Seek Support:** - Lean on your support network, whether it is friends, family, or a therapist. Surround yourselves with people who can provide guidance and understanding.

**12. Celebrate Progress:** - Celebrate your achievements along the way, no matter how small. Recognize the effort you and your partner are putting into rebuilding your relationship.

**13. Avoid Blame:** - Avoid dwelling on blame and guilt. Focus on moving forward rather than rehashing past mistakes.

**14. Reflect on Growth:** - Reflect on the personal and relational growth you have experienced throughout this journey. Use these lessons to strengthen your bond.

**15. Plan for the Future:** - Collaborate on future plans and goals. Setting shared aspirations can motivate you both to move forward together.

**16. Maintain Flexibility:** - Be adaptable as you navigate the changes and challenges of rebuilding your relationship. Flexibility can help you overcome obstacles.

**17. Embrace Imperfections:** - Accept that both you and your partner are imperfect. Embrace your imperfections and focus on growth and improvement.

**18. Renewed Commitment:** - Approach your renewed relationship with a sense of commitment and dedication. Treat it as a valuable opportunity for growth and happiness.

**19. Monitor Progress:** - Regularly evaluate your progress and check in with each other to ensure you are both satisfied with the direction of your relationship.

Rebuilding a stronger relationship after infidelity is a challenging but rewarding journey. With effort, understanding, and a shared commitment to growth, you and your partner can create a foundation for a more resilient, loving, and fulfilling partnership.

# c) Committing to a Faithful Future

Committing to a faithful future is a crucial step in the healing process after infidelity. It signifies a renewed dedication to your relationship and a commitment to prevent cheating from happening again. Here is how to make this commitment and build a faithful future:

**1. Reflect on the Past:**

- Take time to reflect on the events that led to infidelity and the consequences it had on your relationship. Understand what went wrong and why.

**2. Mutual Decision:**

- Make the decision to commit to a faithful future together. This should be a mutual choice made by both partners.

**3. Learn from Mistakes:**

- Acknowledge the mistakes and actions that contributed to the infidelity. Use these lessons as a foundation for change.

**4. Set Clear Expectations:**

- Establish clear expectations for fidelity in your relationship. Define what fidelity means to both of you and what behaviors are unacceptable.

**5. Communicate Openly:**

- Maintain open and honest communication about your commitment to fidelity. Share your concerns, fears, and desires with your partner.

**6. Rebuild Trust:**

- Continue to work on rebuilding trust in your relationship. Trust is an essential component of a faithful future.

### 7. Self-Reflection:

- Engage in self-reflection to identify any personal issues or insecurities that may have contributed to infidelity. Commit to personal growth and self-improvement.

### 8. Seek Professional Help:

- Consider ongoing couples therapy or counseling to address any lingering issues and strengthen your commitment to fidelity.

### 9. Accountability:

- Hold each other accountable for your actions and behaviors. Be responsible for maintaining the trust and fidelity in your relationship.

**10. Set Boundaries:** - Reiterate and reinforce the boundaries you have established to prevent infidelity. Discuss what behaviors are considered breaches of trust.

**11. Transparency:** - Maintain transparency in your actions and interactions. Avoid secrecy or deceit, as these can erode trust.

**12. Practice Empathy:** - Continue to practice empathy and understanding towards each other's needs and emotions. This fosters a supportive environment.

**13. Relish Your Commitment:** - Celebrate your commitment to a faithful future. Acknowledge the progress you have made and the positive changes in your relationship.

**14. Stay Committed:** - Stay committed to your relationship even when faced with challenges. Understand that temptations and difficulties may arise, but your commitment remains steadfast.

**15. Regularly Revisit:** - Periodically revisit your commitment to fidelity. Assess your progress and make any necessary adjustments to maintain a faithful future.

**16. Share Dreams:** - Share your dreams and aspirations for the future as a couple. Collaborate on building a shared vision that inspires both of you.

**17. Support Network:** - Lean on your support network when needed. Seek guidance and encouragement from friends, family, or a therapist.

**18. Celebrate Milestones:** - Celebrate milestones in your journey towards a faithful future. Recognize the effort and dedication you and your partner have put into your relationship.

**19. Renewed Love:** - Approach your relationship with renewed love, appreciation, and a sense of adventure. Embrace the opportunity for a faithful and fulfilling future together.

By committing to a faithful future, you and your partner can build a relationship that is characterized by trust, love, and the shared goal of preventing cheating. It is a testament to your dedication and the potential for growth and happiness in your partnership.

Chapter 12:
Conclusion

# a) The Importance of Self-Awareness and Introspection

In our journey through the complex terrain of infidelity and its prevention, one resounding truth emerges: self-awareness and introspection are foundational to understanding, healing, and building stronger relationships.

Throughout this book, we have explored the multifaceted reasons why men cheat, delving into emotional disconnection, sexual dissatisfaction, personal insecurities, and the allure of opportunity. We have examined the devastating consequences of infidelity, from emotional and psychological turmoil to its ripple effect on children and families. We have offered guidance on rebuilding trust, rekindling romance, and fostering open communication.

However, at the heart of it all lies the necessity of looking inward. Self-awareness is the compass that guides us through the labyrinth of our emotions, desires, and vulnerabilities. It is the mirror that reflects our deepest fears and insecurities, as well as our potential for growth and change. Here is why self-awareness and introspection are paramount:

**1. Understanding Your Triggers:**

- Self-awareness helps you identify the triggers that may lead to infidelity. By recognizing your emotional vulnerabilities and patterns, you can take proactive steps to address them.

**2. Healing and Forgiveness:**

- Introspection allows you to heal from the wounds of infidelity and find forgiveness, whether you are the one who cheated or the one who was betrayed.

**3. Preventing Recurrence:**

- By understanding your personal insecurities and areas of weakness, you can work on them, reducing the likelihood of future infidelity.

**4. Strengthening Emotional Connection:**

- Self-awareness fosters emotional intelligence, enabling you to connect more deeply with your partner and fulfill each other's needs.

**5. Effective Communication:**

- Knowing your communication style, triggers, and emotional responses enhances your ability to engage in effective and empathetic conversations with your partner.

**6. Navigating Temptation:**

- When you are self-aware, you are better equipped to recognize situations that may tempt you and make conscious choices that align with your commitment.

**7. Personal Growth:**

- Introspection fuels personal growth, allowing you to become the best version of yourself and, in turn, contribute positively to your relationship.

In the pursuit of a faithful and fulfilling future, self-awareness is the lantern that illuminates the path. It empowers you to confront your inner demons, embrace your strengths, and embark on a journey of growth and transformation. It enables you to build a relationship characterized by trust, love, and resilience.

Remember that self-awareness is not a destination but a lifelong journey. As you move forward, carry with you the knowledge that the power to prevent infidelity and cultivate a strong, lasting partnership lies within your capacity to know yourself and grow from within. In this journey, may you find not only the answers you seek but also the profound wisdom to create a love that endures.

# b) Empowering Women with the Knowledge to Protect Their Relationships

Throughout this book, we have explored the complex and sensitive topic of infidelity with the aim of providing insights and guidance for both men and women. While understanding the reasons behind why men cheat is crucial, it is equally important to empower women with the knowledge and tools to protect their relationships and foster healthier connections.

Knowledge is a powerful tool, and by equipping women with the information and awareness they need, we can contribute to creating stronger, more resilient relationships. Here is why empowering women in this context is so vital:

**1. Awareness of Signs:**

- When women are aware of the signs of infidelity, they can recognize potential red flags and address them early, preventing further damage to the relationship.

**2. Communication Skills:**

- Equipping women with effective communication skills enables them to engage in open and honest conversations with their partners, fostering a deeper emotional connection.

**3. Emotional Intimacy:**

- Understanding the importance of emotional intimacy allows women to actively cultivate and maintain a strong emotional bond with their partners.

**4. Sexual Satisfaction:**

- Knowledge about men's sexual needs and desires can help women navigate sexual issues more effectively, leading to a more fulfilling sexual relationship.

**5. Building Self-Confidence:**

- Empowered women are better equipped to support their partners in building self-confidence and self-worth, reducing the risk of personal insecurities leading to infidelity.

**6. Setting Boundaries:**

- Empowerment enables women to set clear boundaries within their relationships, which can deter infidelity and promote trust.

**7. Seeking Professional Help:**

- Encouraging women to seek professional help when needed can be a crucial step in addressing relationship challenges and preventing infidelity.

**8. Mutual Growth:**

- Empowered women contribute to the mutual growth and strengthening of their relationships, creating a partnership built on trust, communication, and resilience.

**9. Preventing Infidelity:**

- Armed with knowledge and awareness, women can actively work with their partners to prevent infidelity and address any underlying issues that may lead to cheating.

In the quest for healthier and more fulfilling relationships, empowerment and knowledge-sharing are essential. By recognizing the significance of both partners in preventing infidelity and fostering trust, we pave the way for more harmonious and loving partnerships.

It is important to emphasize that this book is not about placing blame or responsibility solely on one gender. Instead, it is about promoting understanding, empathy, and collaboration between partners. When both men and women are empowered with knowledge, communication, and the tools to build stronger relationships, the potential for lasting love and connection becomes a shared endeavor.

As we conclude this exploration, may the insights gained serve as a catalyst for positive change, deeper understanding, and the cultivation of enduring love in your relationships. Together, we can create a world where trust, respect, and commitment thrive, enriching the lives of couples everywhere.

# c) The Path to Healthier, Happier, and More Faithful Partnerships

As we conclude our journey through the intricate landscape of infidelity, it is with a sense of hope and purpose that we reflect on the path to healthier, happier, and more faithful partnerships. The complexities of human relationships, with all their joys and challenges, are central to our lives, and nurturing these connections is a profound endeavor.

Throughout this book, we have explored the various dimensions of infidelity, from its defining characteristics to the consequences it inflicts upon individuals, families, and society as a whole. We have delved into the underlying causes of infidelity, emphasizing the importance of emotional connection, sexual satisfaction, personal insecurities, opportunity, and temptation in understanding why men cheat.

Crucially, we have also provided insights into preventing infidelity and healing from its wounds. From fostering emotional intimacy and effective communication to rebuilding trust and making a commitment to a faithful future, these strategies serve as a roadmap for couples navigating the challenging terrain of relationship recovery.

The path to healthier, happier, and more faithful partnerships is illuminated by several guiding principles:

**1. Self-Awareness:**

- Knowing oneself is the foundation of personal growth and healthier relationships. Understanding your triggers, insecurities, and desires empowers you to make conscious choices that align with your commitment.

**2. Open Communication:**

- Effective and empathetic communication is the lifeblood of any successful partnership. It bridges gaps, resolves conflicts, and deepens emotional intimacy.

**3. Rebuilding Trust:**

- Trust is fragile, but it can be rebuilt through transparency, accountability, and consistent actions that align with commitment and fidelity.

**4. Empathy and Understanding:**

- Cultivating empathy and understanding for your partner's needs, emotions, and vulnerabilities fosters a supportive and loving environment.

**5. Commitment to Growth:**

- Recognizing that relationships evolve and require ongoing effort, committing to mutual growth ensures that both partners thrive together.

**6. Prevention and Healing:**

- Preventing infidelity through knowledge, awareness, and proactive measures is an essential aspect of building a faithful partnership. Healing from past wounds requires dedication, patience, and forgiveness.

**7. Shared Vision:**

- Collaboratively setting goals and building a shared vision for the future strengthens the sense of purpose and connection within the relationship.

The path to healthier, happier, and more faithful partnerships is not without its challenges, but it offers the promise of profound growth, connection, and enduring love. It requires dedication, self-reflection, and a shared commitment to nurturing the bonds that unite us.

May the insights and guidance provided in this book serve as a source of inspiration and empowerment in your quest for more fulfilling and faithful relationships. Together, we can create a world where trust, love, and commitment flourish, enriching the lives of couples everywhere.

# Epilogue

As you embark on the journey to understand and strengthen your relationships, remember that knowledge is a powerful ally. The challenges and complexities you face are not insurmountable. With dedication, empathy, and the insights gained from this book, you have the capacity to create healthier, happier, and more faithful partnerships.

Relationships are dynamic, and growth is an inherent part of the journey. Embrace the opportunities for self-awareness, open communication, and rebuilding trust. Approach each day with a commitment to nurturing the bonds that unite you with your partner.

Remember that you are not alone in your pursuit of lasting love and connection. Seek support when needed, whether from a therapist, friends, or loved ones who understand the value of healthy relationships. Celebrate the milestones along the way, and remain steadfast in your commitment to building a faithful and fulfilling future together.

May your journey be one of growth, resilience, and love, and may the pages of your own love story be filled with the enduring beauty of trust, commitment, and happiness.

# Why Men Cheat

This book defines infidelity in its various forms, shedding light on emotional versus physical infidelity, and providing a comprehensive list of signs to recognize when a partner may be cheating.

The book delves into the complex reasons why men cheat, exploring the emotional, sexual, and personal issues. Through a compassionate lens, you will discover how these factors contribute to infidelity and what can be done to prevent it.

Written with empathy and understanding, this book is a compassionate guide for anyone seeking to navigate the complexities of infidelity. It provides valuable insights, expert advice, and a roadmap for building trust, commitment, and lasting love.

If you are looking to understand the complexities of infidelity, protect your relationship, or heal from its wounds, "Why Men Cheat" is your trusted companion on the path to stronger, more faithful partnerships.